BREAKING FREE

MY JOURNEY FROM BREAKING POINT AND SELF IMPRISONMENT
TO NEW LIFE FOLLOWING MAJOR PERSONAL TRAGEDY

Brian
wishing you love, joy
and inspiration always
love Anita
xy

Anita Narayan

MOTIVATIONAL PRESS®
LEADERS IN GLOBAL PUBLISHING

Published by Motivational Press, Inc.
1777 Aurora Road
Melbourne, Florida, 32935
www.MotivationalPress.com

Manufactured in the United States of America.

ISBN: 978-1-62865-252-9

CONTENTS

Acknowledgements

Although I have contributed to an Amazon bestseller in the past, this is my first book, and therefore a unique journey that has been full of learning and discovery regarding my inner voice.

This book came to life with the help of some serendipitous events and divine appointments, for which I feel humble and truly grateful.

I would like to say thank you to Geoff Thompson. Geoff, your words of insight and wisdom have been like anchors as I have navigated the journey of self-expression in this book. I continue to feed from those words in my ongoing development as a human being and as an author.

My thanks and gratitude also goes to Ana C. Vasconcelos. Ana, you have reawakened the songwriter within me, and helped me to reconnect with my singing voice after years of suppression. You have been a fellow companion in the book writing process through continuous prayer, and I am richer for the spiritual bond we share.

I am also grateful to Steve Collazo. Steve, despite your fame with the music band Odyssey, your ability to put me at ease during the studio recording process of the song has turned a potentially intimidating scenario into a fun adventure of discovery and expression with my voice.

My gratitude extends to Paul Friend of FACE TV, who helped me put together a video interview. Paul, your generosity of time and resource has been deeply appreciated.

Then there is my long-time friend Wendy Thomas. Wendy, you have a great eye for proof and I really appreciate your objective eye looking several times over each draft of my book. I am so thankful for your help on this aspect of the book creation process, as well as your ongoing belief and encouragement in my gifts.

To all of you who provided endorsements for this book as a result of the inspiration you received, I am honored to have touched your lives to the core. That is the mission of this book and song. This is a dream come true.

Above all I am grateful to God, my Creator, who not only kept me alive so I could bring this to you, but is the source, reason and inspiration for my life.

Anita Narayan

Author, Speaker, Songwriter and Freedom Coach

FOREWORD

THERE IS A GREAT POEM BY THE PERSIAN MYSTIC, RUMI ABOUT A chickpea. Reading it always helps me when the pain of life seems to outweigh my ability to cope. In the poem, the chickpea is being boiled alive in a pot. In a bid to escape he leaps almost over the rim.

"Why are you doing this to me?" he asks the cook.

The cook knocks him down with the ladle. "Don't you try to jump out. You think I'm torturing you. I'm not torturing you. I'm giving you flavour, so you can mix with spices and rice."

The chickpea – realising the divine purpose of his pain - says to the Cook, "Boil me some more. Hit me with your skimming spoon. I can't do this by myself."

When I first read Anita's wonderful book, and experienced with her the seemingly senseless pain and sorrow and grief of her early life, it reminded me so much of Rumi's beautiful allegory. From my experience, God only breaks down those He wishes to build, and He never burns unless there is healing intended.

I believe that Anita is destined for great things, and this book is perhaps the beginnings of that. Not just because she has experienced torment. Every soul has its season of ill. Rather it's because, like the chickpea, she has found spiritual refinement through her pain, and she is using the elixir of that torment to guide, to help and perhaps to save others.

That takes massive courage. And for that she has my greatest admiration. This is an amazing, honest, painful and above all else an inspirational book. I highly recommend it.

Geoff Thompson

Bestselling Author, Screen Writer, BAFTA Award Winner

BREAKING FREE

Song by Anita Narayan

I couldn't see how I could survive, let alone to feel alive inside

As the rubble of my life lay all around, a devastation far too big

All my inner assets were frozen, I was numb from all the endless
trauma

No will to carry on, an endless nightmare, which had no answer.

My prison bars were made of unforgiveness, the guilt and shame,
destructive in their power

So I tried to run and hide from this huge storm, there was no cover

Trapped beneath my grief and all the anguish, afraid to ever love
myself again

I was locked within a prison, and my life, was void of meaning.

Then somewhere in the dark, an inner voice broke through

Through a crack in my closed heart I saw a light

As I looked up in the dark I felt a hand reach out

And in the still surround, I clearly heard….

"Listen to me...

Though you walk through fire you will not be burned

Though the waters rise above you, you will never drown

My grace and strength will shield you, you'll never walk alone

And you will come to know the love that's needed,

In order to break free".

My heart revived I rose out from the rubble, an inner gauge had clicked, I came alive

I went and stood where I had seen that light, I turned to watch myself

Ripple waves of light were emanating, a new strength and a love were burning brightly

And the bars that once had formed my inner prison, they just dissolved away.

As I started opening up my heart a little more, so that inner voice began to speak again

And a new dawn came and took away the darkness, I felt and heard beyond immediate pain...

"Listen to me...

Open up your heart now and you will see the key

Use your intuition now, and you will start to see

Your prison door is open, you can now be free

Choose your path with wisdom, and your vision,

You are breaking free".

And I just kept opening up my heart a little more, and that inner voice grew strong and very clear

I could see a path to living with a vision, with a message written in my life for all....

"It's plain to read now

Settle with your heart now, choose to love yourself

Embrace your gifts and talents, you were born to let them shine

Don't exist but live now, let love flow through you

Bringing life to you and all around,

Help to set them free".

Open up your heart..... you will see the key...reach it with your hand... and you will know, that you are breaking free.

INTRODUCTION

A Wake Up Call

'THINGS CAN CHANGE IN A MOMENT'. THE UNMISTAKABLE VOICE OF MY intuition had spoken like a repeated soundtrack within me. A few days later an unannounced storm of gigantic proportions hit Britain. Days later, the stock market crashed. That was back in 1987.

Little did I realize that this intuitive message was a symbolic precursor to an unprecedented storm that was to break out seemingly unannounced in my own life, although the subtle 'weather patterns' leading to this storm were there long before I knew they were.

May 1992 was the moment my life changed forever. It was a point on the landscape of my life where I was in the final year of my psychiatric nurse training, and it should have signified the final lap of that course. I felt secure, if not entirely free from the effects of what life had personally delivered so far.

That night I had a dream that shook me to the core of my being. It foretold and revealed two contrasting themes - a devastating life event that would leave me feeling destroyed, and an inspirational journey that would set me free. When I awoke I could not see past the dream's revelation of the terrible impending life event.

Shortly after the traumatic awakening left by the dream, the foretold devastating event took place on home soil, plunging my life into prolonged turmoil and despair. Somewhere in the aftermath of the event, I pulled the threads of the inspirational clues from the dream into my life, and went on a journey that surpassed healing and survival.

That journey brought me to you. If your relationship with yourself feels anything but deeply loving, journey with me and read on. If you are feeling anything but alive on the inside then continue to read.

May the message and the journey of this book and song reconcile you with yourself in a deeply loving way, in such a way that breathes new life into you, and inspires you to translate that life into powerful and authentic self-expression, the substance of which true dreams are made.

Many blessings,

Anita Narayan

PART 1

THE STORM

"When you come out of the storm, you won't be the same person who walked in. That's what this storm's all about."

Haruki Murakami, 'Kafka on the Shore'

Storm Clouds

...44 years earlier, Bury St Edmunds, 1971

Signs of Turbulence

My parents were from the tropical Fiji Islands, and their parents were from India. My entry into the world was humble and less tropical. I arrived in this world during the harsh winter of 1963 in Pratt Street, Camden Town, London.

Up to a point my childhood seemed happy enough. After all I had a roof over my head, food in my stomach, and a school education. I was the second of three children. My earliest memories of myself were of a child infectious with laughter, full of the joy of life, and eager to explore life.

I liked helping others and spoke out when people were treated unfairly. I was quite an independent little explorer, brave and free spirited, wanting to explore the world like a little Christopher Columbus. Somehow, that independence shielded me in part from the emotional poverty that grew increasingly visible in my family.

I loved school, and although I was bullied for the color of my skin, it did not stop me from enjoying my school days. At home things seemed fairly normal, apart from bath time, which was strangely unpleasant.

I was scrubbed so hard it felt like I was being cleaned with a scouring pad. Teeth were not deemed to be clean unless the gums bled, according to Dad. Hugs were rare in our family. The language of love very much reflected duty, obligation, and responsibility, rather than warmth, intimacy and nurturance. This seemed fairly typical of Asian culture.

I seemed to be born with a natural love and talent for football. In keeping with my brother's favorite team, I soon became an Arsenal supporter – strength or vulnerability? You decide.

Football talent   *Laughing at life*

I was also far more attracted to boy's activities than girl's activities – a right tomboy! I got far more thrill from playing football, having piggy back fights, and cycling in the dip of the woods while getting muddy in the process, than I did from playing with dolls, knitting, or dressing up.

The sedentary, passive nature of girl's activities seemed boring compared to the adrenaline flow and excitement I felt from the more mobile, physically engaging, and high tempo activities that seemed to be the domain of the boys.

School reports from an early age consistently mentioned my cheerfulness, love of football, courage, and willingness to help others. Some of these qualities were soon to become a thorn in my parent's side, so to speak. For example, they did not mind me playing football within the private confines of family life, but were against me playing publicly with the boys.

My Mum and Dad appeared to be hard working, although I could never work out why Mum had to work permanent night duty as an intensive care nurse. Dad was working in the chemicals industry, except I noticed that he was more at home than at work as the years proceeded.

So it was Dad that took us swimming, Dad that took us to the park to play, Dad who initially spent more time with us. Dad was my closest relationship, but I missed Mum being around.

I can remember when Mum was on a day off and cooking in the kitchen, I would stalk the kitchen like a lion marking its territory, and would constantly tug and hold onto her skirt so I could keep close. If anyone as much as entered the kitchen and came within two feet, they would be greeted with a defiant scream. It was not exactly a gracious greeting, yet that was the effect of having so little time with Mum.

Somewhere after the age of 7yrs, I recall running with Dad to catch a bus one day to visit Mum in the hospital. I did not realize that she was having an abortion, let alone understand why she would need to abort her fourth child. We were living in St Albans at that time, and had been there since I was three years old.

My initial fears were that Mum was not very well or that there was a serious medical problem with the pregnancy. I remember thinking it must be serious for Mum to have to go to this length, as she had given birth to three children before that, and it all seemed well planned.

My visual recall of anything immediately prior to or after her hospitalization is virtually blank. My only recall of any explanation given about the abortion, was that it was due to severe financial difficulties. As far as I knew Mum and Dad were still working their respective jobs, so the explanation only raised further questions in my mind.

The theme of financial difficulty was to resurface again. I was eight years old and living in St Albans when I picked up this sad feeling in the house. I also remember Mum and Dad having heated exchanges in the kitchen. I soon learned that we would have to move to a smaller property due to financial difficulties.

That was all I was told. I was to discover the underlying roots to the financial stress in an abrupt manner when I turned 11yrs old. I did not want to leave St Albans. I loved it there!

The day we moved to Bury St Edmunds in March 1971 was very depressing for me. It marked the start of much heaviness in the house. Something else was wrong though, but I just could not work it out.

THE STORM BREWS

....41 YEARS EARLIER, BURY ST EDMUNDS, 1974

SHOCK WAVE 1 – VIOLENCE ERUPTS

BY THE TIME I WAS ELEVEN YEARS OLD, IT HAD BECOME PRETTY ROUTINE that every time Mum gave us pocket money, we ended up giving it to Dad. We were told he needed it due to financial difficulties. Something did not quite add up though. How was fifty pence pocket money going to make a difference to his financial situation?

After persistent inquiry, I soon learned from Mum that Dad was using the money to feed a compulsive gambling habit he had developed since the day my brother was born. Mum discovered this when the money put aside for food shopping kept disappearing from the kitchen. When she confronted Dad he was not forthcoming with the truth at first, but eventually confessed he used it for gambling. He was stealing money to feed his habit.

Over time, an uncle ended up bringing bags of food to the house to ensure we were catered for during the losses incurred. Mum was later to explain that she had a difficult decision to make – to keep all three children fed, or to risk having a fourth child and struggle to feed us all. My father's unrelenting addiction had left her with a horrible decision to make, and one which I know she struggles with to this day.

We were to give our pocket money to dad to 'keep the peace' due to his increasing aggression. His compulsive habit would explain the fuss he made over fifty pence.

I decided not to give Dad the money. I believed that if I gave Dad my pocket money I would be contributing to an addiction that was making him 'sick'. My hope was that he would understand the conflict and accept my decision as a loving and caring response.

I don't know who got the biggest shock - Dad, because I said 'no', or me, because his eyes turned wild like a man who was possessed. Dad threatened to kill me in ten minutes if I did not give him my pocket money when he returned.

One thing I grasped very quickly was that he meant it. His eyes told me so. The wild look in his eyes disturbed me, and I remember thinking, 'one day your bubble will burst and I don't know if I will like it when it does'. Now I understood why Mum wanted us to hand over our pocket money to keep the peace, and I can understand why the others did. For some reason I chose not to give in.

Shortly before this event, my parents had introduced us to a practice called Transcendental Meditation. This mind technique comes from an ancient Vedic tradition in India. The idea is to spend about 15minutes daily in silence, focusing on a mantra or sound given by the instructor during an initial meeting. You repeat it quietly in your mind. The mantra is like a vehicle for helping to quieten the mind to a more relaxed and aware state.

My parents had come across this while searching for something to help my brother with his stress levels. My brother would suffer from major headaches and migraines, and get visibly stressed very quickly, when dealing with daily matters. My parents considered we could all benefit from the practice.

Dad quickly turned this into a discipline that we had to carry out daily, otherwise the rod was there to beat us into submission. How anyone was supposed to meditate and get the benefits of meditation in that environment, God only knew! I felt about as relaxed as a porcupine.

However, I took some refuge from meditating and the new lease of energy I experienced. So when Dad threatened to kill me, all I could think to do was to grab the cardboard sign I had made for meditation, and hang it on my bedroom door - it said 'do not disturb'

How naïve was I to think that this could stop anyone from coming in. My father seemed to have the rage of a bull. At least the sign was in green, not red!

The one thing I did not grasp at that tender age was my brave decision to refrain from supporting Dad's gambling addiction, even if I died!! Was that courage or stupidity manifesting?

And so the longest ten minutes of my life played out, seemingly in slow motion. I don't remember meditating during that time. I just sat on the edge of my bed, and every noise in the house seemed amplified. My heart was beating wildly as I sat in anticipation of my final moments on this earth.

The Cord Gets Severed

Dad did not come back as he had threatened. In fact he left the house and did not return till later that day. However his attitude toward me had changed dramatically. He virtually blamed his gambling losses that day on my refusal to give him my 50pence pocket money. It was as if I had betrayed him.

He did not attempt to force money from me physically and while my life was spared on that occasion, my father let me know verbally that he could take my life any day, and that he would destroy me over time, as long as I continued to deny him my pocket money.

It is one thing to threaten to withdraw love in the absence of money. It was another to threaten to withdraw someone's life. That threat took things beyond mere emotional blackmail to terrorism. It was frightening.

The change in the relationship with my father felt like the severing of a cord. He became emotionally cold toward me and dismissed any attempts to reconcile with him. He started to disown me, excluding me from family conversations and plans. He barely acknowledged my presence in the house, except to heap more domestic chores and place heavy social restrictions on me. I was treated like a traitor.

As I continued to deny him money for gambling, my life became more about physical survival as violence visited my door regularly till the day I eventually left home.

And still I did not give in.

We were later introduced to church by our parents, as part of the process of turning us into good citizens. It was strange to be welcomed so warmly by people I hardly knew. It was also pleasant. I did not grasp that it was possible to have a personal relationship with God, as I believed that the only access to God was through organized church gatherings.

That being said, the miracles described in the Bible fascinated me so much that I loved going to Bible studies during the week. These were held in someone's home only a few doors away from our house. I started to find myself waking automatically at 4am on a regular basis to pray, which was intriguing, because I have no recollection of any conscious decision to do so, and it was unusual for me to wake up before 7am. I don't even recall the specifics of my prayers beyond trying to connect and petition God for my safety and the wellbeing of my family.

I noticed that anything resulting in a new sense of joy was cancelled out by further abuse and recrimination from my father. The God of the

Bible did not seem very active in my life. Maybe he was on holiday. It must be tiring to look after the whole world.

What was miraculous was that I remained happy and joyful for the next three years, at least to the outside world. My humor and joy for life seemed to shield me to the growing trauma playing out in my family life. I seemed to be able to smile in the face of pain. Nobody knew anything was wrong, and my parents were viewed as the charming couple to the outside community.

From 11years old I was stripped of a lot of privileges. For example I was banned from going to Bible study. I was stopped from playing football publicly, yet I was allowed to continue to play competitive tennis, along with hockey for Club, County and East of England. I was told that girls do not play football.

More emphasis was put on academic study and domestic chores, and I seemed to be given more than my fair share of chores. Most of these restrictions came from my father. These restrictive rules were connected significantly to the decision to withhold money from my father. It seemed like he really wanted me to suffer as a result of that defiance.

The Bible study group had given me a sense of belonging, adventure and refuge that animated me. My father must have noticed that I seemed to be finding something fulfilling outside of the family environment.

Maybe he guessed I was also confiding in this group about what was really going on in my family. I was banned within weeks of attending this meeting, and my departure was marked with tears by some within the group.

At some level it was still very confusing. After all it was my parents that made us go to church in the first place. Why encourage me to go to church and play football as a young child only to invalidate and disallow it later when these activities came to have deeper meaning for me?

It seemed that my parents had a definite female image they wanted to mold me into. They also had a definite career type in mind for me too, which had high status as the defining factor, such as a solicitor, doctor or manager.

Asian cultural values may have played a part too. I felt at times that they were trying to preserve their cultural norms in a western society. In Asia the emphasis was on loyalty to family, duty, obligation and responsibility. Problem-solving through discipline and action was deemed more valid than emotional availability.

Academic success was imperative. A child was expected to deliver on achieving high grades, no matter what, and females were treated in a more subservient manner. The prospect of arranged marriages would be mooted occasionally.

It seemed that when I was not fighting to stay alive at the hands of my father, I was being forced to live out an image of a female and work toward a career lifestyle that I did not own. My life was being mapped out for me and I did not like the direction it was taking, but I had very little say in the matter at this point.

At some level I think my parents wanted the best for me but it was shrouded with so much conflict, possessiveness and disempowerment that I felt like a slave under someone's dictatorship.

I started to question the point of my life. What was the point of trying to stay alive in my own family? What was the point of living someone else's version of life? What was the point of living when I didn't fit in and could not be myself? My enthusiasm for life was starting to weaken.

Maybe that is why I went to extreme lengths to keep engaged in the one activity where I felt alive. That activity was football. It was particularly painful the day my father banned me from playing football in public, and not just because I was good at it.

As much as I loved sports in general, I was truly in love with football. For me it was the beautiful game. It was the one activity which took me beyond mere enjoyment and display of talent. I felt alive and free. So I played behind my parent's back.

Football started to take on a deeper significance for me after the dramatic decline in the relationship with my father.

For example, I remember when I was at middle school that some of the male teachers would join a group of us at break time whilst we played a match. Sometimes they would kick the ball with me one on one. At other times they would watch and comment on my talent with great enthusiasm and validation.

The boys in the team loved my participation and treated me as an equal. I was then invited by my teacher to play in the boy's football 'house matches'. This was an internal school competition where pupils were assigned to one of four house groups. Each group would compete against the other across different sports.

I was the only girl to be asked and the boys in my house team wanted me to play. There was one problem though. I had to get my parent's permission in writing for reasons to do with safety policies. I was not given permission, and so I decided to create a parental signature. The school seemed to accept this without double checking, so I got away with it!

It was a truly amazing experience to have my inclusion in the boy's team treated with huge celebration by everyone. My talent was not just acknowledged and encouraged. It was embraced without reference to gender. I was treated as a person in my own right.

From this one scenario alone, it was as if football was holding up a mirror of life before me, where I could be myself, and express my gifts and talents without judgement. The teamwork I experienced created harmony and gave me a sense of belonging.

There was no condition, stereotype or prejudice attached. I had never experienced such unconditional positive regard. Football held therapeutic value too because I was able to discharge tension in a positive way and successfully channel all my emotional pain into great performances on the pitch. So I lived for football, and I believe it saved my life, as it helped me to hold onto life when I felt my grip weakening.

School became something of a refuge too, as well as a fun environment. It gave me the freedom to explore learning and to dream of a future. I had dreams of getting married one day, having three children, having a loving family that would be hospitable to others, and owning an enterprise through which I could do something really big to help others in a humanitarian context.

When I wasn't at school, I felt like I was walking back into a prison. I was constantly reprimanded for the way I looked, the way I spoke, who I kept company with, and what I wore. My parents did not approve of me wearing trousers a lot and jeans were banned, something I have made up for in later life. I ended up doing more cooking at home too, which felt like penance.

As for love, that became increasingly transactional where my father was concerned. I continued to refrain from giving Dad money, knowing that it was for his gambling. Dad continued to let me know that any day he could take my life and destroy me.

For most of the time I suffered in silence. My brother, sister and mother were not party to all of those events, because Dad seemed to save his more aggressive behavior for times when he and I were alone.

Even so, every now and then the extent of the conflict and violence from my father would become visible to the family, but I think they were so absorbed in their own survival battle, trying to keep the peace in the face of marital arguments and potential violence, that they felt powerless to help me as well.

The three of us would watch through the back window whenever we knew Dad would be returning from the betting shop, in order to gauge his mood from his body language. Depending on what we saw, we either ran upstairs to our bedrooms to keep out of the way, or we stayed downstairs to enjoy the rare moments of good fortune and good mood.

Dad developed a new twist to his unpleasant behavior when formal spelling tests were introduced. My brother and I were made to compete against each other as Dad fired verbal questions at us. We were tested against each other, and although neither of us liked this, we had no choice. I always seemed to come out on top, and unfortunately this invoked jealousy in my brother.

How else was he supposed to feel at that time? We started to fight, and grew apart as the comparisons and tests intensified. I hated what Dad was doing, and neither I nor my brother had the emotional resources to cope and overcome without fighting each other.

We often fought until blood was shed. It was another horrible conflict arising out of my father's controlling behavior. I constantly felt broken hearted about the destructive 'divide and rule' approach that Dad took toward us as a family.

At home, life was a constant battle between remaining true to myself while staying alive. I lived with great restriction, yet tried to maintain some sense of self.

My father was also extremely possessive. If I hugged a male friend, he would wake me up early the next morning to question whether I was in a relationship with that guy. If I hugged a female friend, I was supposedly gay. If I hung out with anyone disabled, I was lowering my social standards.

I was also banned from talking to anyone outside of home about family issues, because white people could not be trusted according to Dad. If I laughed a lot, my father criticized this as abnormal. If I cried, it was deemed weak.

Nothing I did seemed to fit my Dad's idea of who I should be, and how I should behave. Mum and Dad tried to present a unified front in our upbringing, but they were clearly at odds with each other when it came to certain values. Mum tried to balance things out, but at times it was clear that her loyalties were divided.

The arguments between Mum and Dad escalated over time, with increasing violence from Dad directed at Mum. Often at night time, my brother, sister, and I would hear thudding against the wall from downstairs. It was extremely distressing to hear, and I would make up an excuse to go downstairs in the hope of interrupting and stopping the violence.

Dad saw through it though, and would redirect his anger toward me. Still, I would stand between Mum and Dad, and take the resulting verbal or physical abuse, in the hope that Mum might be spared in part or whole.

For all the abuse I suffered from my father, I was at least spared the horrible abuse of rape. My father was sexually inappropriate toward me on three occasions, and I feared a new wave of abuse was about to start. They all happened in close succession.

One day I was sat in the lounge reading. I must have been about 14years old. Dad bought up the subject of arranged marriages and asked what I thought about the idea. I said I was not interested.

He persisted with conversation and then proceeded to show me how boys kissed girls. I was taken back and pulled away very quickly. On another occasion I recall Dad lowering his trousers in front of me to reveal a rash near his groin area. This was also strange as Dad was quite private and never exposed his body other than when we went swimming, when he was quite appropriately in swimming trunks.

On the third occasion I was in my bedroom, alone and tearful because I felt miserable and in fear of what each day would bring from my father. Dad walked into the room, and for a moment seemed to forget how horrible he had been toward me.

However he suggested that my behavior and poor relationship with him was down to being unwell. He promised to send me on holiday for a break anywhere I wanted to go, and proceeded to roll me back on the bed and hug me.

Nothing happened but his groin was pressed far too tight to me for comfort. At the same time he suggested I visit his family. When I suggested I would like to go to another country where no-one knew me, the offer was withdrawn abruptly, and he physically retreated.

Mum must have passed by the bedroom door during that episode because she was very emotionally cold toward me for a few days, which only reinforced the discomfort I had felt.

I did wonder if this sexually inappropriate behavior was part of a possessive trait endemic within our culture, as the other sexual abuse came from an indirect friend of relatives who was of similar culture. I had gone to stay with Dad's sister and family in Luton.

The husband worked in an Indian food shop and I was helping out one day. One of his colleagues then informed me that he wanted to check if my breasts were real and proceeded toward me. Nobody responded with any alarm except me. I was ready to hit the guy somewhere very appropriate! However, I managed to get physical distance before I could be groped or things became dangerous.

I noticed on another occasion that two of Dad's sisters had bruises and a black eye. I suspected that domestic violence and abuse were an accepted part of the control exerted on families by men in our culture; such was the passive acceptance these women expressed whenever I tried to get to the bottom of what happened. The cumulative effect on me was that I became more withdrawn at home.

I started to do my homework later and later into the night after the arguments had died down, when my parents had gone to bed. It was not uncommon for me to study between one and three o'clock in the morning. Eventually this pattern took its toll.

At school I had started to confide in my religious studies teacher. She seemed quite astute in her observations that all was not well with me beyond my apparent physical tiredness. It took some time for me to open up to her as I was afraid of word getting back to my family.

She assured me of confidentiality and seemed to show deep understanding of the dynamics of family life. She was very academic in the way she relayed things. Still, she was very supportive and kind, and it was comforting to have someone to talk to. As violence escalated at home, she invited me to use her home as a 'bolt hole', or alternative study environment, if I was able to get away for a while.

In spite of the support, I found myself falling asleep during class in school. This eventually became a cause of deep concern for the teachers despite my best efforts to hide the reasons behind my fatigue. It appeared I was leaking distress, if only through my physical demeanor. My religious studies teacher became more worried for my welfare too.

I was summoned to see the deputy head, and with great reluctance I told him the truth behind my fatigue. At the same time I pleaded with him not to call my parents in, as I knew that they would class this incident as a betrayal of the family culture, with severe consequences for me.

Unfortunately, the deputy head thought he knew better, and called my parents in to talk to them. My life got worse from that day. I was now seen as the 'black sheep' of the family, a betrayer of family values and someone who was not to be trusted.

One morning I found myself going to school, and in usual fashion went to the library to get some studying in before classes. However, instead of sitting in the main part with others, I found myself retreating to a less visible section of the library. I did not want to talk to anyone. I went from a person with vibrant energy to one with constant fatigue. The plug on my energy had come out.

From that day onwards I went from a bubbly, sociable person to a withdrawn, sad figure. It was as if all the events from the age of eleven years old had caught up to me as a fourteen year old, like an inner thermostat had gone 'click'. Now I had reached the limit of how happy I could be. It had taken prolonged and systematic abuse to bring me to this point, but now I felt burned out.

One night at midnight, I remember leaving home with two bags, never to return again. I wasn't sure where I was going, but knew I had to do something to make sure I stayed alive. With hesitation, I found myself going to the home of the school teacher I had confided in She accepted me in without question, and due to the lateness of the hour, helped me get to bed.

The next day I went to school with her, and later found myself being summoned to the office of the year head. I was told to apologize to my family and return home. I was shocked and horrified that I was effectively being blamed for my home situation. I felt betrayed. It had taken me everything to pluck up the courage to reach out when it would have been easier to keep quiet.

I was dropped off home by my religious studies teacher. The drive home was in silence on my part. Her silence during the journey seemed apologetic, yet she did not express any objection to what had taken place earlier. This made me feel angry and betrayed by her too. It seemed like the person I had confided in had not persuaded the year head of the true situation. Our relationship from that day onwards became strained.

That same day I told myself I would never trust another human being again. The punishment at home became relentless and I felt like I was on my last legs, dragging myself through my studies to pass my 'O' level exams.

My father did have a tender side to him, and I remember an occasion which demonstrated this, as well as how quickly he could change for the worse. For example, I remember when I was in the first year of my 'A' level studies. I was 18years old. One day I felt like something was in my eye causing intense pain. I had never experienced nerve pain before and this felt horrible. For twenty-four hours I felt sick and vomited at the sight of food. I was then admitted to the hospital and quarantined for two weeks whilst receiving medical treatment, after being diagnosed with shingles in the right eye.

I had to take two months sick leave from school whilst my right pupil was dilated for rest, which meant having to wear an eye patch. During the first couple of weeks, I witnessed the tender side of my Dad. He fed me, made me drinks, sat with me, and bought me two of my favorite music albums. He even allowed my religious studies teacher to visit me at home. Why did I have to be ill to experience such basic nurturing?

A couple weeks into my recovery I saw how quickly his behavior could change. My two records had disappeared, and I learned that Dad had sold them for money. Mum and Dad were then having a customary argument about their marriage, and Dad asked us all to comment and give our opinion. We were not allowed to opt out.

I spoke my truth as I saw it. I was outspoken when it came to injustice. At the core of what I communicated was that I could not understand how Dad could blame Mum for their marriage issues, when his gambling addiction was at the root of the problem.

Furthermore, I could not accept his hitting Mum, because hitting people to control them and extort money from them was not a sign of manhood. I am not sure which part of my opinion was responsible for the next act of violence - blaming Dad or challenging his manhood. I suspected the latter. My words had clearly hit a nerve that he could not handle because what followed next happened so quickly.

The full force of Dad's swing of the hand left my head spinning and ringing. There was something very calculated too, because of all the places he chose to hit me, he picked my right eye, the one that had recently been affected from shingles. There was immediate bloodshed.

I turned around like someone who had nothing to lose anymore, and told him in a rather venomous fashion that if he ever hit me again I would call the police. Furthermore, I decided I would return to school the next day, against medical advice, even though I could not read properly.

The quick change from tenderness to robbery and violence was too much to bear, and I was reminded that it was unsafe to be at home more than I needed to be. As much as the physical pain in my eye was unpleasant, it did not compare to the underlying emotional pain that Dad's actions inflicted.

Upon my return to school, my tutors wanted me to redo the first year of my 'A' levels, because I had missed too much course work. They considered it to be technically impossible for me to pass my exams. However, I refused. I was desperate to leave home and told them I would just do my best.

I broke it down in my mind. I had decided on becoming a Physical Education teacher and opted to apply to Bedford College. I knew my parents did not approve of my choice of career, but I stood my ground. Sport was the one thing I strongly related to and this seemed to be the closest related degree.

I had three subjects to pass – Religious Studies, French and English. I needed three E grades as minimum pass marks. I had to drag myself back to school and somehow achieve what seemed impossible according to the teachers.

A Spiritual Rebirth

Shortly after my bout of shingles, I seemed to have what I can only describe as a spiritual rebirth, which resulted in a personal and active belief in God. I had resumed studies at school.

One day, some sixth form friends introduced me to their church, a more community type charismatic church compared to the more established orthodox churches. The family atmosphere gave me a sense of belonging, and I started to witness some miraculous answers to prayer amongst this group as a result of the faith and belief that was evident. There was more emphasis on a personal relationship with God, rather than organized Christianity. It reignited a sense of life and adventure in me as well as a sense of refuge.

I developed a couple of close friendships on both the male and female side. I became prayer partners with one of my best male and female friends from that group, and always looked forward to our weekly get together.

My new found faith in God seemed to cause more threat to my father. He sat me down one day and stated that he used to be able to control my mind until I actively started to believe in God. What a strange comment, and quite delusional I thought. Still, anyone who could loosen the control of my father on me was a friend of mine. God just became my best buddy!

A new wave of recriminations followed as a result of this, including not allowing me to go and visit my mum after she underwent a hysterectomy in a hospital seventeen miles away. Though I managed to find a way around the threat, the constant battles were wearing me down and my energy was dissipating. Then my first personal miracle happened.

In my heart I had been praying that I would defy the odds my tutors had given me of getting through my 'A' levels, and that I would pass my exams. It seemed an impossible request. I didn't care what specific grades I got, I just wanted to pass.

This would be my ticket to physical education teaching college, which would then allow me to leave home legitimately. Did I really want to become a Physical Education teacher? I had no idea. All I knew was that I loved sports and wanted a way out of my home.

It was hard to read properly, and there was much discomfort as a result of reading solely out of one eye at first. On recovery, I continued to play hockey for club, county and East of England. My prayers to stay alive and pass my exams became incessant.

Then the miracle happened - I passed my A levels the first time! I couldn't quite believe it. I had scaled my first mountain by making the impossible possible. It seemed that God had heard my prayer and had come to the rescue.

What was so incredible about this was that I had to rely on my left eye for reading, as my right eye had felt so weak. This was not helped by returning to school against medical advice. The subjects I was studying involved a lot of reading too.

For example, both English and French did not just cover technical proficiency with the language. It also involved reading a lot of literature which consisted of no less than twelve books. I was on catch up as a result of my two month absence. What frustrated me was that I could not read with any speed due to the state of my eyes.

I studied for very long hours and prayed before each session that my eyes would hold out, and that I would be able to memorize key points despite the distracting pain that coursed through my head as a result of nerve inflammation in the eye.

I do recall picking some key topics on each subject that might appear in the exam. I practiced answering them. It was a bit risky to be so selective but I had to take a chance or risk superficial revision.

On the day of the exam I could not determine how well I had done. It was too stressful and I felt like I had waffled with imprecision in my answers to the questions posed by the exam papers. But there was no doubting the piece of paper I held in my hand now, confirming that all three subjects had returned a pass.

The tutors were amazed, especially as they had not given me any chance of passing. I now had a ticket to leave home. Dad's response at my results was deep disappointment that I had not achieved any 'A' grades. I had gotten used to this by now, but it still hurt. Why did I hope that he might change? It only ended in painful rejection at every turn.

I could tell you that at that point I stopped wanting his love and approval, and that was what I decided in my mind. In my heart I suffered with my decision.

What I had learned though was that it was not safe to be in my own family. I would soon learn that it was not safe to be in church either.

THE STORM GATHERS MOMENTUM

...34 YEARS EARLIER, SEP 1981 – JULY 1982

SHOCK WAVE 2 – AN INNER IMPLOSION

WHEN I WENT TO COLLEGE I FELT A GREAT SENSE OF RELIEF. I SAW MY opportunity to establish a career, stand on my own two feet, and break free from the need to depend on my parents in any way. However, what I had not counted on was the sickening fear that remained because of not knowing what might be happening to Mum after my departure.

Would she now feel the full escalating force of a man who was controlled by a compulsive gambling habit that dictated his mood, and from which he could change quickly and fire up into a rage?

On this note it would have been easier to be at home. If I was there at least I could know what was going on and intercept if necessary. Here, I was left to imagine, and it was harder than I thought it would be.

I felt like I had abandoned someone in trouble. That abandonment played out like an inhibiting force at college, cancelling out any sense of enjoyment at my new found freedom.

Still, I did my best to compartmentalize things so I could take advantage of my new freedom. I bought my first guitar, and found that I started to write songs from inspiration based on my spiritual awakening.

They were songs based on the theme of love and strength in adversity. They went some way to shielding me from the pain of wondering what was going on at home. I also remember experiencing another miraculous event, after I attended a spiritual boot camp on the topic of faith. I

---

attended this camp with a college friend during a bank holiday weekend.

On the day of return, what we did not know was that there was no public transport available from Cambridge to Bedford, and I had to get back to Bedford College for an exam at two o'clock that afternoon. There was a transport strike. It was now nearly midday, and Bedford was thirty miles away.

I knew instinctively that we were being tested on the very topic of faith we had learned about at camp. I suggested to my friend that we go to the outskirts of Cambridge, and said I believed we would get a lift. I had never hitch hiked before for safety reasons, but felt strongly that we should and that we would be looked after.

Twenty minutes later a lady pulled up in her car and offered us a lift. She appeared a little nervous, quite understandably, and explained to us that she did not usually stop to pick up strangers. When we asked where she was traveling to, it turned out that she was due to visit her husband in Bedford prison, which just happened to be next door to Bedford College. Amazing!

We arrived back at college with five minutes to spare. The driver had been glad for our company and the opportunity to offload some of the difficulties surrounding her circumstances. We thanked her for her kindness, and let her know we would uphold her in our prayers.

As time progressed my body started to manifest viral type fatigue which I could not keep at bay. I continued to play and excel at hockey for the college, yet my body felt like it was crumbling, and I felt it most of all in the recovery time after a match.

Then, as if hit by an unseen force, something happened to me one day, which would quickly bring me toward a nervous breakdown!

It started with a young man I met through the college Christian

Union. He was your everyday guy who was studying for an agricultural degree near Bedford. He was of medium height, slim, dark haired, with rugged looks. He was dating one of my friends at the time, but that ended a few months later.

In the interim, we became good friends and prayer partners. We played squash. We wrote to each other during holidays too. His honesty of heart and hunger for spiritual growth touched me deeply. He was candid about his struggles too. Over the course of many months I fell in love with him. I wanted to marry him and create a family of three children with him.

What I was not expecting was that somewhere in tandem with this I began to experience increasingly strong feelings towards a woman.

She was one of the college tutors. In fact this tutor had interviewed me for a place at the college, and on reflection, something about her demeanor intrigued me during that interview. She had these gentle eyes that exuded kindness and compassion.

Those eyes seemed to hold me and look deep into me with genuine interest. She had this calm, assuring tonality that was coupled with an aura of serenity and grace that I rarely witness amongst professionals. She walked with purpose and presence.

She was beautiful on the outside too. She was fairly tall and slim with long dark hair which was always tied back. She had dark eyes too. When I shared my spiritual beliefs she smiled knowingly so I guessed she was a believer too. I felt drawn to her and intrigued. That was as far as I processed things on that occasion because I was just so thrilled to be accepted to the college. On reflection I think she had me at 'hello'. I just did not realize it at the time.

When I started college I would see her passing by on occasion. She always noticed and acknowledged me, and was concerned to know that I had settled in well.

I felt this increasing strong pull toward her. I noticed with greater curiosity how she maintained this air of grace and serenity about her in a hectic college environment.

A few days later I was having lunch in the college restaurant, and shortly after, she entered the hall to have her lunch. I just remember feeling excited, nervous, and overcome with this deep love I never knew was possible.

She was beautiful from the inside out. I could not believe it, yet I could not deny it. I had fallen in love. I had no idea that love could reach such depth and height. It was so multi – dimensional. Every cell in my being felt alive with such vibrancy I had never known before. I had never felt so captured by someone's presence as I felt now, and it stopped me in my tracks. I simply sat and gazed on for what seemed a long time. The rest of the day was something of a blur. I found it difficult to concentrate on my studies, and was relieved to get to the end of the day.

That evening I could not work either. I was gripped by the strength of these feelings, yet horrified at the same time. How could I be in love with a woman? How could I be in love with two people at once? What's more, the feelings I experienced towards this woman were undeniably so much more three dimensional and powerful. As for the man I had fallen in love with, I didn't love him less. It was simply a case of a more expansive love experience toward this woman.

I felt trapped between a shattering dream and a new emergence of feelings. I was confused by my sexuality and had not seen this coming. Sure, I had experienced some fleeting feelings towards women in my teenage years, but thought this was part of an adolescent phase.

I recall having a crush on one of my female school teachers. It was something about the gentle feminine energy that would draw me in. Sometimes, though less so, I would experience a crush on a man. On the occasion this happened I noticed that he would have a nurturing demeanor about him. Clearly emotional availability combined with tenderness and kindness were ongoing themes that were not simply the domain of women. The feelings I experienced would be intense, yet temporary.

However the experience with this female college tutor was so different. Even though I knew she was married with children, the feelings I had grew stronger and more enduring. It was not just about the qualities I described earlier. It was about the interplay between those qualities, and the soft subtle physical and emotional touch of this woman. Ironically as a teenager I used to dream about a love expressed like this but always felt I was fantasizing. Now that dream was playing out for real, albeit in one sided fashion.

I found myself in great emotional turmoil. As beautiful as this was, at a more conscious level I did not want these feelings. It only reflected back to me the possible painful rejection of not fitting in with societal norms. I had suffered much rejection in my family. I needed some aspect of my life to feel simple and uncomplicated.

Therefore I wanted to marry the man I loved, and have three children with him. Had he asked me to marry him, I would have done so at that time, in spite of these new feelings.

His close friends would remark about how we had this special connection. They felt he should date me, and every signal I seemed to receive that this might happen appeared to be a positively confirming one. However nothing came of it and one of his close friends seemed to think that he was afraid. I will never know

Nothing happened between me and the female college tutor either. My love toward her was undisclosed and experienced in my heart alone, from a distance. But I had been stretched to a new dimension of feeling and there was no going back, as hard as I tried. Every time I attempted to suppress these feelings, they kept resurfacing with undeniable force.

Not only was I confused about my sexual orientation, but I could not reconcile this with my spiritual beliefs at that time. I had found solace and belonging in the church and knew their traditional stance on sexuality. I knew the church would deem my emerging sexuality as unnatural, morally wrong, and unacceptable, and I had adopted this belief.

I decided that if I was capable of falling in love with a man, maybe I could rediscover these feelings by praying for my feelings toward women to go away, whilst redoubling my efforts towards my relationships with men.

I wanted to be able to talk about it, but at our Christian group meetings my peers would laugh mockingly about the subject when it came up in general discussion. So I kept silent and suffered in silence. I felt trapped between the need to be true to myself and the need for acceptance and belonging.

I had already been rejected at home, and found a new sense of belonging through church. How could I suffer further rejection from the church and from God?

However, the more I prayed, nothing seemed to change. If anything, the feelings towards this woman became more pronounced. Something had been awakened, and like Pandora's Box, I could not shut it. Maybe collective prayer would uproot this infestation.

I decided to confide in the pastor of my home church near Bury St Edmunds. The response was to deliver me from demons through prayer. I didn't care how they labelled this. I just wanted to be free from these feelings so that I could realize my dream to be married to a man and have children.

I was disappointed when nothing seemed to change from collective prayer either. If I gave into my feelings I was going to hell according to the church's interpretation of the Bible. The conflict was too tortuous. For the first time in my life, my need to belong and be accepted overrode my need to be true to myself, so I compromised authenticity.

I suppressed my feelings, remained true to my faith as instructed by traditional church teachings, and prayed incessantly to recover some sense of attraction towards men.

By the end of the college year I felt so ill. The suppression and denial had taken its toll. My studies had suffered. I could not concentrate. I felt horribly exhausted, and depression was settling deep inside. The thought of what might be happening at home to Mum, coupled with the tortuous journey concerning my sexuality, shattered my energy, resulting in a nervous breakdown.

In the privacy of my room I cried uncontrollably for days without any sense of relief. Days of crying turned into months of crying without relief, and my jaws ached badly at night - I did not see a doctor though. I felt too ashamed. I could not study any more.

I left college after one year, feeling ashamed and defeated. I returned to the family home out of concern for Mum. I was about to re-enter the lion's den, so to speak. I took on an administrative job at the civil service in the benefits department and later tried my hand in my first entrepreneurial post selling Kirby vacuums.

It was a heavy piece of technology, and appeared quite tall beside me. The vacuums had a special filter which would show the dirt that came off carpets and mattresses, even after the consumer used their own vacuum. I was too busy consoling the prospective customer after this revelation when I should have been more focused on hammering home the need to purchase the Kirby. So I failed quickly and miserably at this venture.

However, entrepreneurial seeds had been sown.

Meanwhile, Dad's addiction to gambling had escalated to the point where he had resorted to even more fraudulent means to get his hands on money. He had forged signatures when dealing with the banks, and by the same method extorted money from Mum's account.

Mum decided to divorce him and I assisted her. It was an ugly process. However, what made things significantly worse was that soon after the divorce, Dad had persuaded Mum to let him back home, and to my horror she did just that – Dad could be mighty persuasive.

Mum started to effectively blame me for the divorce. She spoke as if she had misjudged Dad in the light of his apparently reformed behavior. She talked as if I had influenced her into the divorce. It seemed that Mum did not want to acknowledge and accept how bad things had been with Dad.

Mum's love for Dad appeared to reflect in denial. It would blind her at key moments to his manipulative and abusive behavior. Dad was so good at the 'divide and rule' behavior. He only had to turn on the charm and claim he had changed, for Mum to believe him. Mum did not seem to have the resourcefulness to see beyond or combat that because I think she wanted to believe that he was still the man she originally married. All the same, divided loyalty was an on-going theme in her life, and its impact on me was disorientating and destabilizing.

When Mum and my siblings were not around, I suffered a new wave of abuse. One day I was given an ultimatum by Dad. He declared that now that he was back at home, I either did what he said or risked being destroyed. A furious row broke out and I decided I had no choice but to leave, or I might not survive this cycle of abuse.

Mum heard the row and came downstairs. She had been sleeping after doing a night duty. As I approached the front door Mum challenged me as to why I was behaving awkwardly now that Dad had changed for the better.

The denial, deceit and betrayal felt like a final blow. I did not even reply, but quietly went out the door into the night, never to return home again. I stayed at the home of some church friends for a few months until I had saved enough deposit from my job to move into a bedsit, and then my own flat.

For the next couple years when I bumped into family in town, they barely engaged with me. I did not try to persuade them otherwise. I knew Dad had sold them a lie, and maybe for them the truth was too much to bear. Everyone has their own way of surviving. They were going to have to come to their own conclusion. Still the rejection weighed heavily on my heart.

THE STORM BREAKS

SHOCKWAVE 3 – DEATH

ON AUGUST 16TH 1984, I WAS IN MY FLAT PLAYING MY GUITAR AND praying. I was twenty-one years old. I had this strange inkling all day that something very testing was going to happen. Psalm 23 kept going through my mind like a record on continuous play.

Later that afternoon Dad turned up at my flat in Bury St Edmunds. I knew it must signal bad news because Dad had never visited me since my departure from home. He briefly announced that my brother was really ill in the hospital and I needed to be there. He still could not resist telling me to change my clothes before I left. You guessed...I was wearing trousers!

Mum worked as a night duty ward sister on the Intensive Care Unit at the local hospital. My brother had been urgently admitted to the same unit on her day off. By the time I arrived on the ward, I found my brother strapped to a life support machine. This machine kept him breathing. His hands were stone cold. Nothing was making sense to me. He had no recognized illness beyond the migraines he had suffered during his teenage years.

I was informed by the doctor that he had suffered a massive brain hemorrhage. My mother understood the significance of what was being said. I had no clue and started praying fervently for his recovery.

Blood had gone from his brain and flooded into his chest. The doctors were unable to drain his chest quickly enough. Later that day he was pronounced dead. He was only twenty-three years of age.

The cruel irony was that he was on a simulation exercise with the Royal Air Force, where his role was to play dead for that week!

The only diagnosis offered on further tests was a suspected congenital aneurism. In layman's terms he was deemed to have had an abnormally large artery in the brain from birth that was susceptible to bursting under extreme stress or head trauma.

As I looked up from his hospital bed through tears, I saw my father eyeing Mum and others in the room in a strange and suspicious way. I did not know what was going on in his mind, but his behavior seemed odd and out of context to the tragic event that was playing out. That look stayed with me and disturbed me.

The grief felt unbearable. I had lost my only brother, and several months before he died, our estranged relationship had started to improve. The turning point was when my brother personally witnessed Dad's fraudulent action.

My Dad had persuaded my brother to lend him his credit card under false pretenses. My brother naively handed it over. At the end of that day Dad returned, having taken and lost £1000 on a gambling spree. With a clinical tone, he simply told my brother that Mum would return it – no feeling of remorse there whatsoever.

This was the day my brother awoke to the truth of what was going on. But his stress levels had increased dramatically and continued long after the event. He and his wife had been expecting a baby in March 1984, so were saving money.

Their son was born in March. The acrimony between my brother and Dad continued intermittently until his untimely death in September. My grief was accompanied by anguish and guilt.

Had Dad's behavior tipped my brother over the edge, or had the manner of my final departure from home become a stressor? How could my father cause so much devastation in his own family? Could I have saved my brother if I had stayed at home longer? I would have gladly died in place of my brother so he could enjoy a life with his wife and son.

I felt tormented and devoid of comfort. Not long after I was to have my closest shave with death when I contracted a virus that left me quite ill. I had been working at a chicken factory. For two nights I had a fever and could not move. When the doctor finally came out and took some blood tests, I discovered that my blood count was so high I could have died. I don't think I cared at that point.

I was ordered not to engage in any physical or mental exertion for six weeks. During that time I stayed at a friend's whilst they were running a church camp. I was under medical supervision. During that stay, I met a Christian family who would become like another family to me - more on that later.

I suffered insomnia for several months after my brother died and had this constant paralyzing fear that I would wake up dead. I could not shake this, and I lay in bed at night wide awake from the terror this fear induced. It eventually subsided and disappeared after six months.

After I recovered, I decided to leave Bury St Edmunds and get away. I got a job as a relief manager for a chain of newsagent stores in London, in January 1985. This meant getting up at three o'clock in the morning and often not getting back home till nine o'clock at night. It suited me fine. I did not want to think about my grief.

During that time I lived in Wimbledon, London, and shared a house with some church friends. I learned the hard way that time is not a healer unless you do something to process that grief.

After six months I quit my job as I finally acknowledged the need to deal with my grief properly. I got another job with Wandsworth Borough Council in their rating and valuation department. A seven hour day felt like part time compared to the previous six months of eighteen hour days!

I started to attend a community church and played hockey for Wimbledon. I continued to deny my sexuality, but it reared its head again when I started to experience strong feelings towards another woman. She was one of a group of four females I shared a house with in Wimbledon. We were all practicing Christians. She was very affectionate, kind and caring. She was a willing listener, and had a gentle, compassionate demeanor about her. We developed a very affectionate bond, and while I did not fall in love with her, I was strongly attracted to her.

Again nothing happened, except that I continued in denial and suffered. I knew the church would also disapprove, and no amount of prayer on my part changed anything.

I did eventually pluck up the courage to tell her and she was very gentle about the way she responded to me. Her response was very much in line with traditional church teachings. Homosexuality was seen as a sin, but it was a case of loving the sinner not the sin, so her rejection was not personal. She was very sensitive in the way she handled me.

I would see men I liked but was unable to feel more beyond a general affection. Meanwhile, I was finding it hard to come to terms with my brother's death and the stressful events that led up to that moment. If I thought this event was the last of the storm, I was to get an even more horrifying wakeup call years later.

In the meantime, to many of my friends I seemed strong. I was labelled as one of life's survivors, strong and always looking out for others in spite of what might be going on in my world. I am glad to say that this part of me remained intact. However the relationship with me was quietly going downhill. I was consumed by a quiet but definite self-loathing.

In the late autumn to winter I contracted an acute virus of some sort. One night I woke up in the early hours of the morning unable to swallow properly. I felt like I had a golf ball stuck in my throat. I was so frightened that I called a friend the next day, and asked her to pray for me.

Overnight, I went from playing club hockey to not being able to cross the room without feeling like collapsing. It was a frightening experience and when I visited my doctor, he took some medical tests which returned a diagnosis of Myalgic Encephalitis.

Back in those days very few knew of its existence let alone believed it to be a legitimate illness. Basically I had suffered an acute viral attack on my throat, which then left my immune system fighting long after the acute symptoms had subsided, hence the physical exhaustion. Every muscle in my body was in pain, and sleep did not feel refreshing, hence I slept a lot!

Some months later, the Christian family I had met earlier near Bury St Edmunds invited me to come and live with them. I had become very much like family to them, and they felt like family to me too, which was a scary admission for me to make.

I knew I needed some lengthy time out to recover from this illness without being alone, as I felt too ill to look after myself. This was a strange feeling after having managed on my own through far more serious events. It was frightening to feel in need of human help, yet I felt broken!

One of the first things I was confronted with on return was the death of one of my close male friends who had been a previous prayer partner. He drowned after experiencing an epileptic seizure whilst canoeing. He died on the same ward as my brother, two years after my brother's death, and this bought up unresolved grief concerning my brother.

It seemed that key significant males in my life were disappearing. Now, on top of everything else, I had this irrational fear that anyone who got close to me would die, so I became more socially withdrawn!

In April 1987 I moved in with this Christian family in a village near Bury St Edmunds. Those next three years were to be significant in terms of healing. I was surrounded by a family of six. The children became very much like brother and sisters to me.

It was during my time of living with this family that the full extent of the damage to my self-esteem became apparent to me. When I wasn't helping out with practical chores, I would virtually apologize for my presence and go to my room. Nobody asked me to; in fact the family loved my presence and enjoyed my company.

Unfortunately I was unable to appreciate what they saw in me. I felt a burden to myself and others. The children would wander why I slept in till one o'clock in the afternoon. They would shout up at the bedroom window from the garden, wondering when I was going to come out for a game of football.

Their teasing of me and their light heartedness was probably the best remedy for my state. It took me two years to start to feel comfortable around people again, and let go of previous conditioning, but eventually I started to resurface…and we played lots of football!! They were also a very musical bunch so we played and sang lots of songs, including the ones I wrote!!

I went to church with them and found some benefit, but it was constantly offset by this gnawing shame about my sexuality. Only the parents of the family knew this about me. I could not tell the children, as I feared their rejection.

I tried dating a guy on one occasion but failed miserably after a few months. We had met at work. I was 26 years old. We were both working for a warehousing company. I was an account manager. He worked in the warehouse assembling orders for the companies I serviced.

He was small, slim, fairly shy, and a very kind man. He was a true gentleman as far as manners went too. I liked him and he liked me. We became close over a period of months. However I wanted to feel more toward him than I actually did because of his qualities. I was still in denial about my sexuality.

I genuinely loved him, but not so much in a romantic way. However I thought that if I tried harder maybe other feelings would come through more strongly. He asked me out. I accepted and we started dating. He did not know of my inner struggles at this point. We kissed but I never went to bed with him.

At best I could only feel warmth and affection. I could not feel any great arousal beyond this. He was kind enough never to force the issue, but eventually we talked about our relationship. I decided I needed to tell him about my sexuality.

His response was very kind and understanding. He also thought that if I tried harder I would feel more intimacy toward him. If only he knew just how hard I had tried, and if only it were that easy! I ended up breaking off the relationship and breaking his heart, which felt horrible. He didn't give up on me, and the only way I could get through in the end was to be really emotionally cold with him, which felt like such an unkind and desperate strategy. This only added to my self-loathing.

I suffered one more relapse of Myalgic Encephalitis that year, albeit this one was short lived compared to the previous one – six weeks instead of six months. It was to be the last bout I had before the virus left my body permanently.

On recovery, I decided to go travelling with the son of the family I lived with. We went to New Zealand and Australia, stopping off at Hawaii and Fiji. Unfortunately I felt obliged to visit Mum and Dad's side of the family who lived out there.

Any ideas I had that my father's side of the family would be more accepting of me, were dashed in a moment when my relatives gathered round me and offered me a house in their garden, an arranged marriage, and a job! Under normal circumstances I might have accepted! I rapidly declined the offer, much to their disapproval.

I was later to learn that my father had orchestrated this discussion and had instructed his family to try to 'bring me back in line'. That night my cousin had confided in me that she had been taken by her parents to Fiji, supposedly for a holiday, only to find herself forced at knife point into an arranged marriage.

I slept on my passport that night as I did not wish to expose myself to the risk of being kidnapped and forced into an arranged marriage!!

All in all the time spent living with the Christian family had been a significant healing period because of the love that surrounded me. The storms life had dealt seemed to be subsiding now, and I felt strong enough to resume a more independent life and a new career.

In 1990, I left Bury St Edmunds to embark on a three year training diploma in mental health nursing in Basingstoke. I had previously wanted to enter the police force as a detective; such was my fascination with the mind and problem solving. However back then a female had to be 5ft 4" and I was only 5ft 0".

So my fascination with the mind, and my humanitarian outlook, took me into the field of psychiatry and mental health. Little did I realize that I was going to call on my training and related skills for reasons unexpected and unwelcomed.

THE STORM REDOUBLES

...23 YEARS EARLIER, BASINGSTOKE, MAY 7TH 1992

SHOCK WAVE 4 – THE WARNING

I woke up suddenly at dawn, shaken by a powerful dream, not knowing its true meaning. Yet somewhere deep within me I knew that what I had dreamt about was not fictional or the mere processing of a day's activity.

The dream revolved around an autumn scene in a harvest field. It involved a young woman who was grieving heavily, a toddler, and a man who sets fire to the field to destroy everything and everyone in the field. It also involved a great rescue by an unlikely animal.

Instinctively, I knew I had received a warning with limited time to unravel the message. I was due to attend my clinical community placement that sunny day in May 1992, as part of my psychiatric nurse training, and so I did. However throughout the day I felt like I was in a bubble, relatively detached from the outside world.

'When you become still, the answer appears'

Thomas Edison

The external noise and voices of people seemed distant and mute compared to the impact of the dream I had. I was deeply troubled. I wanted to be alone and back in my room in the nursing home to seek insight into this dream. The day seemed to drag, but eventually I got back.

Thomas Edison once said 'when you become still, the answer appears'. Little did I understand the power of the process I was engaging with at that moment. I just did it instinctively.

I asked the question out loud as to what this dream meant and sat in silence. Within ten minutes the answer became clear… and then horror took over.

The message of the dream snapped into place like a gridlock within a moment. It just seemed to bypass my logical mind and present itself in a complete picture in a three dimensional manner within moments. In essence it reminded me of the following scripture:

Isaiah 43 v 2-3

'When you pass through the waters I will be with you, and when you pass through the rivers they will not sweep over you. When you walk through the fire, you will not be burned; the flames will not set you ablaze'

I share the full contents and interpretation of the dream in the second part of this book. For now, without hard evidence or clear details, I knew that a devastating event was about to unfold, and that somehow it involved my father, as the perpetrator. The dream revealed another theme and message. It foretold that even though I would feel destroyed in the wake of the event, I would not be. It alluded to a specific inner journey that would happen in the aftermath.

Little did I know at the time that the dream I had was well after the event, and that I was to uncover something which had already taken place from further back in time. I was in the final year of my nurse training and went through the rest of the year with barely three hours sleep a night, as I tried to piece the finer details of evidence, working back from the dream.

One day that summer, my mother visited my sister and me. This was very unusual for her. In similar vein to the day my father visited regarding my brother's hospitalization, I knew this visit would not be a carefree one.

Mum appeared lifeless during her visit, like someone who had taken one knock too many and had no energy to go on. When she recounted the on-going events and abuse at home, there was something she described that disturbed me and only underlined my worst fears.

Mum had been asleep following a night duty shift at the hospital. Dad entered her room and woke her up to ask for money. Mum declined. A wild look unfolded in Dad's eyes, as he threatened to kill someone for money and kill himself in the same breath.

It was this wild look described by Mum which disturbed me because it reminded me of the same look that had greeted me at eleven years of age. Only this time, with terrifying force, I felt that Dad had either just done something terrible or was about to do so.

I strongly advised Mum to consider divorce for the sake of her life. I had no idea that she had re-married dad after her first divorce, until now. It turned out that the basis for that re-marriage came when Dad turned up on her doorstep one day with my nephew.

He declared that my nephew's mother had allegedly asked my parents to raise her child, as she wanted to go abroad with a new boyfriend. Dad sold Mum the idea that my nephew needed a mother and father to raise him up, and they then got remarried on that basis. Little did mum know that once again she was being used as cover for a horrible event.

This time I had no intention of getting directly involved in a potential divorce, due to being blamed for the first divorce. I also knew my family was in danger, but I had to tread a difficult path as I was alone in that belief.

By the summer, through a process of intense deliberation, I had come to a horrible conclusion. I was convinced that my father had murdered my sister-in-law, and that she had not left the country in the manner stated. I still had no hard evidence to support this, and the weight of my conclusion was beyond agonizing. But Mum's description of Dad's behavior with his wild look, coupled with the fact that nobody seemed to know where my sister-in-law was, only strengthened the intuitive insight from the dream.

Initially, when I sounded it past my family they threatened to disown me if I pursued my conclusions regarding my father. They could not comprehend that he might go this far to secure money, and felt my mind had gone too far. This would not be the first time I had been cut off, and the thought of further rejection felt like a sharp knife to a healing wound. I would have to take that risk though, as I knew I was not wrong in my conclusion, and lives were at stake here.

I did confide my fears with a couple in the church I was attending, and they supported me with their prayers. I could not tell anyone at nursing college, as I had no proof, but that year was one of the loneliest years I have ever encountered. When I eventually spoke to someone it was my personal tutor, with whom I had developed a great trust and respect.

He listened with an open heart and mind in my hour of need. Over the months, he would often support me for hours on end, listening to me unburden the tortuous thinking and conclusions I had arrived at. In fact he was one of few who believed me without reservation, before the evidence presented itself.

It was he, who further taught me to face the difficult questions in life with an open mind, where others would look the other way. He remains a rare human being who has impacted my life personally and professionally beyond the event in question. He became a close friend to me and we still keep in touch to this day.

———

For the most part I encountered people who were more unhinged in their rational state than I was in my trauma – you know the ones - those who seek to destroy what they cannot understand, and in their mind consign you to a team of psychiatrists!!

Over time, when I sat down with my mother and sister and separated what they knew for a fact, versus what Dad had told them, I grew increasingly horrified as my worse feelings became corroborated. My family was now beginning to question things more deeply.

In one conversation with my sister, when we traced back events to the last time my sister-in-law was seen, everything pointed to her not going abroad, and the conclusion we reached was that there was no evidence that she had left her home. It was then that we became convinced she was buried in her garden. I felt sick and wanted to throw up at this point, but still I had no hard evidence.

Even so, I urged the police to look there first rather than chase all the dead end leads they were given. I think they thought my mind had gone into overdrive, and I became increasingly frustrated. One of the practical issues was that the house in question had been sold when Dad remarried my mother, so the police felt they had to have a solid reason to go in and seek permission to dig up the garden.

However, September marked a turn of events. Mum had instigated divorce proceedings and the court then asked for my nephew's mother to come forward to have a say in his custody hearing.

This was the first time anyone had officially asked to know where my sister-in-law was. Dad was supposedly the last person to see her, so I decided to ask him where she was, so that we could bring an end to a bitter divorce as quickly as possible.

It was his answer that was to start to give him away. When I asked my father where my sister-in-law was, he told me she had gone to a certain country, yet had told the rest of the family that she had gone elsewhere.

When I confronted my father about the discrepancy, he denied giving conflicting stories, but something about the way he looked at me told me everything I needed to know. My heart felt sick as the unfolding of the dream became more evident.

Fortunately the brother of my sister-in-law registered her as a missing person. If he hadn't I would have done so. The police inquiry began from that moment, and we were required to give police statements. I told the police what I thought had happened, and I am not sure that they knew how to handle what I was telling them.

At the same time Dad also refused to give Mum a divorce, alleging that she had had an affair. His ludicrous and desperate attempts to discredit Mum in order to claim financial compensation were predictable and callous. My sister and I had to produce affidavits for the divorce hearing.

One night in October, my mother nearly collapsed on the ward during her night duty. She later informed me that on the same evening she was eating a meal Dad had prepared, prior to getting ready for work. Mum was due to start another stint of night duty. She described the meal as if it had excess salt, and added that it tasted extremely bitter in places. Later that night on the ward she nearly collapsed from pain. Her nursing colleagues were immediately on hand to help her recover.

Mum's blood pressure was already excessively high and controlled by medication. There were times during this period that Mum was forgetting to take her medication due to the combination of stressful divorce proceedings, Dad's volatile behavior, and the quest to find my sister-in-law. My instinct told me that Dad was attempting to aggravate her blood pressure towards fatality, to try to create an accident. I believed his behavior was now escalating in view of the police inquiry.

It was as if Dad thought he was invincible. In my mind I knew what I thought he was up to. If he could make Mum's death look like an accident by aggravating her blood pressure to tipping point, he could then make claim to her will.

Something took over me at that point in spite of the potential danger. I went straight home and asked to speak to my father in private. I asked him to grant Mum her divorce without contention. He refused.

He had that wild look in his eye again, but this time I held his stare and said I would see him in court. I added that he was not to expect my affidavit to favor his case, as I would have to tell the truth.

As I turned round to leave, I also told him that I was aware of his violence and scheming toward Mum. I warned him that if he physically harmed Mum after I had gone back to nursing college, I would be back!

Mum rang me later that night when I arrived back at college, to ask what I had said to Dad in private that evening. My conversation had apparently left him subdued and a pale. When I told Mum, her response was that something about the audacity of my confrontation and the authority within my voice had left Dad looking unnerved, not for the first time either. For Mum's sake I was glad.

The last time I ever spoke to my father was that December, when I was asked to take care of my nephew for a couple of weeks. My father had kept me away from my nephew for many years, so this was an unusual request on his part - a sign of someone who knew his days were numbered as far as I was concerned.

My parting and last words to my father were, 'why do I think that we are about to have a big can of worms opened?' His only response was 'you never ever gave me a chance'. He could not hold my eye contact. I think that was as close to a confession as I ever got.

My heart was constantly filled with dread. Maybe, just maybe, someone would wake me from this nightmare and tell me it was all just a horrible dream, or that my interpretation of the dream was way off, but no-one did, and then the inevitable happened.

A Very Violent Storm

.....22 years earlier, Bury St Edmunds, January 1993

The Event

I had just qualified with a nursing diploma in December 1992. How I managed to pass my final exam with only three hours sleep a night for seven months, God only knows. I managed to celebrate my graduation and also celebrated my 30th birthday with a group of friends, knowing that this was to be overtaken by news of a horrible nature, but determined not to be robbed of marking my special moments.

Days later all hell let loose. I felt the full force of the emotional sucker punch that left me in a fragmented heap. At 5:30pm one afternoon in late January, I received a phone call on the hospital ward where I had just started my nursing career. I was only three weeks employed when the announcement was made. It was the same policewoman who had interviewed me back in September. Her words, 'it happened just as you said it had', were like the final thrust of a knife through my heart.

The words were surreal, yet in that moment all color drained from my face. Everything around me seemed to fade. I didn't know what to feel or how to feel, such was the shock that coursed through my body and inner being.

The body of my sister-in-law had been found under the patio where my Dad used to live. Two hours later it hit the regional news on television. I felt like every part of me was collapsing fast and shattering into thousands of pieces en route.

In January 1993, my father was arrested for the alleged murder of my sister-in-law. She had in fact been dead since December 1986, but the discovery was not made until now. For me, the dream was the turning point of its discovery. It was believed that she was probably strangled to death first.

I sometimes wonder if the acute virus I suffered back in 1986, when I woke up at night unable to swallow properly, was symbolic of what might have happened to my sister-in-law around that time.

The apparent motive for her murder was money! My brother had been working in the Royal Air Force and had a benefits package that his wife would acquire in the event of his death. This included an insurance policy worth approximately £70,000.

I learned from my family, that from the day my brother was dying in hospital my father was scheming to find the life insurance papers so he could work out how he could get his hand on the money. That explains the strange look I saw on his face when I watched him across the hospital bed where my brother was dying that day.

It seemed my father had wormed his way into my sister-in-law's life, under the guise of a supportive grandfather to a widow and single parent. At some point he had moved in with her and they moved to a house at the end of a cul-de-sac. A huge wall had been built during that time.

Police investigations revealed that Dad had managed to send forged letters in her name to her parents, saying she did not want to have anything more to do with them, or us. She had no employer so no-one would be asking questions from work. He had isolated her physically and emotionally. At some point he had secured the house in joint names, constructed a patio in the garden, and when completed, carried out the murder.

By the time the body was discovered under the patio where my father had lived, the remains were bones. Every part of her body had been dismembered, as if done with rage. Forensic analysis was needed to identify her, and the same person who conducted the forensics on the Lockerbie disaster conducted this one. My sister-in-law was positively identified. It turned out she was also pregnant at the time of her death.

I had discovered the truth before the police had – a combination of the spiritual guidance via a dream, the skills I had developed in psychiatry, and processing information with my family to work out its meaning over a period of six months.

It was not until the end of December 1994, after repeated cancellations of the trial and two years later, that my father was imprisoned for murder. He was given the minimum life sentence of fifteen years. Strangely enough, I remained relatively intact for two years and continued to work until the conclusion of the trial.

Nobody knew anything was wrong (except my employer at the time, who was obliged to know), unless they gleaned it from the media. I seemed to contain my emotions privately without it affecting my day to day functioning or performance at work.

I learned something about myself during this adversity – a bad day at the office for me was equivalent to the average person's good day, such was the height of my minimum baseline when it came to functioning and performance.

I was somehow able to show great mental reserve and emotional consistency to the outside world. On the inside I was suffering though, and I could not trust anyone easily after previous betrayals.

I had been acquainted with grief through the death of my brother, enough to know from experience, that the immediate aftermath up to the funeral is a time when there are practical arrangements to be made. Practicalities and shock can have a numbing effect on painful reality.

Strangely enough this distracts from the full force of grief. It is several weeks afterwards when things go quiet, that the real impact starts to register.

However there was something uniquely different about this type of grief. My brother was adjudged to have died of 'natural causes', though there is nothing natural about dying at twenty three years, in my opinion. Yet this current bereavement revolved around his wife's murder by my father, leaving my nephew orphaned. I could not get my head or heart round this.

The loss of privacy via the media and mainstream news was hard to bear, especially when facts were misrepresented in the name of an exclusive story, with all the trimmings of sensationalism and drama that seemed to be the hallmark of media reporting.

We had new things to face, such as the vicar only praying for the family of my sister-in-law at the funeral. This was the same vicar who took my brother's funeral. We also had to get used to others along with the media classing us as 'guilty by association', with all the vitriol and anger that was directed towards us as a result. Even the police found it uncanny that my instincts about the murder turned out to be accurate.

At the trial, Dad fired every barrister that represented him and chose to represent himself. Sadly his case revolved round character assassination. He was aggressive in his questioning of Mum and my sister. However when it came to cross questioning me, he declined to question me or challenge my statement. For some reason the silence of this moment felt like the ultimate rejection.

Dad maintained his innocence, contending that we had conspired to put him in prison. He was found guilty of murder by a jury, and given a minimum life sentence of fifteen years. The rest of the family was left to face the media onslaught.

Damage From The Storm

....20 years earlier, April 1995, Basingstoke

The Aftermath

For some time after the trial, Dad tried to track down my sister through her workplace – my sister was a qualified barrister. Furthermore he sent me a letter stating his innocence, and saying that the reason why he did not cross question me, was that my brother had instructed him in a dream not to, and would help dad find files that would clear his name!!

This felt beyond insulting to my brother's memory, that my father should resort to such behavior and use my brother against me, even in death. I felt this strong inference that Dad would seek revenge if he got out.

In tandem with this, the media was relentless in its pursuit of a dramatic and sensational story, even if they misreported the facts. The rest of our family was criminalized by association in the press and television. This was a new experience, and an eye-opener into the true workings of the media and mass behavior.

There was no respite and nowhere to hide. It seemed that our information and personal lives were no longer ours. I started to feel detached and depersonalized as if I was looking at the outside world through a bubble. Nothing felt real, although it was all so horribly real.

The residual echo of the event was like a cyclone that threatened to take me under. Even though it seemed I had been spiritually prepared for this day via the dream I had, it did not take away from the shocking reality. I continued to experience waves of shock well after the event as if it all kept happening afresh, leaving me disorientated and completely floored.

I was now in free fall, too tired to grab a foothold on anything, feeling unprotected from the emotional blows that were hitting me at every level, and feeling a raw pain that I could not express.

Questions started to pound incessantly in my head like 'why wasn't my love for my father enough to stop him resorting to murder?' and 'if you can't be safe in your own family where can you be safe?'

What was the point in living if he was going to come out of prison one day and resume his murderous intent? What was the point of getting the dream well after my sister-in-law got murdered?

I held myself responsible for not having the dream, or finding out earlier, even though it defied logic. Depression started to set in deeply.

Although I would never have classed myself as someone that would ever consider suicide, my mantra became 'death would be a sweet release'. Psychiatrists would refer to that as a state of passive suicide. In other words I wished to die, without acting on those feelings.

While I was aware of the complex nature of my grief and depression, I could not account for the insidious turn and fresh feeling of blackness that enveloped me one day. When I eventually dragged myself back to the doctor I discovered I had been suffering from an underactive thyroid for four months, yet no-one from the surgery had informed me of my blood test results.

The shortfall of the hormone thyroxine had upgraded my experience of depression, and had it been left much longer, I'm not sure whether I would have walked off a cliff or had a heart attack first. The thyroid impacts both mood and metabolism, which puts a strain on the emotions and heart respectively when not in balance. Needless to say I changed my doctor.

My energy had now changed from free flowing to sluggish, especially in the morning. Now I had less fluid energy from which to tackle some of the biggest challenges in my life!

Counselling was the main therapy at that time, but I barely had the energy to talk when I wasn't nursing. More importantly, I never felt I was getting resolution or any tools to help me progress. I got fed up of constantly reciting how I felt, and left counselling.

The only thing that had medicinal value for me at the time was the words of my new doctor. She did not rush for the prescription pad, and said to me that she had no answers, yet somehow she would help me through this trauma.

Some of the wisest words are simple yet profound. I have never forgotten those words! I tried art therapy in view of my difficulty talking, but the facilitator annoyed me with his controlling style. He seemed to want to interpret my feelings and experiences for me rather than help me define them for myself, so I left.

I did acquire a wise friend, through a charitable organization who focused on supporting the families of the perpetrators, something that was outside the remit of Victim Support. She seemed to have a sensitivity and ability to navigate between words and silent companionship. That was a blessing!

Although I could cope with individual company I could not handle going to support groups of that nature too much, as it only seemed to keep the memories alive for me rather than help me heal. I did not know exactly what I needed right now, but I wanted to be alone.

The thought of getting through the day intact seemed like the journey of a thousand miles. The combination of high standards of care delivery, a murder trial that got cancelled three times over two years, and a thyroid that was no longer supporting free flow of energy, had taken its toll.

I felt generally detached from things around me as if I were watching the world through a misty veil. I did not feel like a whole person, but rather like some fragmented pieces of me hanging together.

I also knew that the one person I needed to help the most was my young nephew, who was now orphaned. Mum now had legal custody, and my sister and I were to help in his upbringing until he was old enough to be independent.

I resigned my nursing post in psychiatry in April 1995, burned out by the combination of a three year protracted process whilst nursing patients with acute mental illness. I simply had nothing left to give.

It's often when you completely stop that the full force of what is going on inside starts to surface. And so it did with me.

To add to the layers of fresh challenge, I now had financial challenges from the fallout of the trial. I had never been in debt before, but the repeated cancellation of the trial three times in two years, outstretched any compassionate leave and sick pay entitlement that could be used. I was broke and on government benefits for medical reasons relating to my thyroid.

I could not imagine waking up feeling happy to be alive again. My mantra intensified, 'death would be a sweet release'! Each morning was marked with a horrible realization of the event I wished were merely a bad dream. I was still experiencing shock waves and trauma, with no sign of relief.

A close friend of mine gave me some money so I could get away for a week. I have never forgotten this act of kindness.

When I came back, I plucked up the courage to share the torment around my sexuality, with some elders in the church I was attending. I felt I needed to address this issue which had been on the backburner in the light of more heavy weight events. While the church elders were kind enough, their response was that I had demons that needed casting out, which they proceeded to do.

When I later reported that I did not feel any different or healed, and that my feelings towards women felt even more strongly established, their prognosis was that I had to remain celibate for the rest of my life or I would be excommunicated from the church and end up in hell. No clarity needed there!

Up till now for the best part of fourteen years, I had denied myself any sexual relationship, putting my need to belong to the church and acceptance of their truth above my need to be true to myself. I could not hold that tension any more. After all that time something in me now snapped. Two things added to this effect.

First of all I had heard that a young man from my home village had committed suicide, as a result of discovering he was gay, presumably because he could not reconcile his religious beliefs with his sexuality. This shook me to the core, and made me question whether anything was worth being destroyed over.

I then spoke to a male friend of mine, whom I had originally met as a colleague during my first nursing post. He was gay but very accepting of his sexuality. We spoke at length, and amongst the many things he said, he gently challenged me as to how God's unconditional love and desire for our wellbeing and happiness could exclude someone just because that person was gay. I had no answer.

These two events were a turning point for me. I was going to have to remain true to myself even if it meant going to hell, as the church believed, and even if my life was to be cursed as a result of my departure. I lost a lot of friends.

That day I left the church before they could kick me out. My relationship with them and God was severed. It took me back to the child who at eleven years saw her relationship with her father severed. This one felt even worse, if that were possible.

The last time I ever sang one of my songs I had written, was in September 1995 to a church gathering of some three hundred people. It was the last time I sang or wrote another song for a very long time.

I felt like I had failed God and had been banished from his presence. I felt that God must now hate me, and I felt on my own. The few remaining props in my life were now taken away – no job to distract me to keep some outward attention, and no church to belong to.

I walked out from church that evening into the dark of the night. All I could see now was the scene of collateral damage, the residue of the agenda of a man that loved money more than family, and a church that wanted to sterilize itself of anybody who deviated from normal stereotypes.

My world had collapsed and as I looked on at the 'rubble' of my life. I felt destroyed. I was alive but dead on the inside.

THE EYE OF THE STORM

...28 YEARS EARLIER, BURY ST EDMUNDS, SUFFOLK

A MESSAGE FROM THE STORM

I WILL NEVER FORGET THE 15TH OCTOBER 1987. IT WAS DURING THE TIME I lived with the Christian family mentioned earlier. I was driving home from work in Suffolk, when a distinct message cut across everything that was going through my mind. The message was 'things can change in a moment'

Where were you on that day, when one of the worst storms to hit Britain came unannounced? It seemed more like a hurricane. I recall waking up at five o'clock in the morning, to see trees scattered on the ground and the roads, making the journey to work the next day impossible.

This storm was severe and devastating in its impact on lives and the countryside. As I watched the devastation and impact, I was also left to reflect on the message of the previous day. A few days later the stock market crashed on the 19th October 1987. I had not been privy to the news or weather forecast, but as far as I can recall no indication was made of either of these events.

First the storm, and then a few days later, the stock market crashed. Now the message I had received came back to me with full force. Why had I received that message?? Was I given a gift of intuition? What was the purpose of receiving this? I certainly could not do anything about what happened.

I recall reading about storms and in particular the eye of the storm, which is deemed to be the safest place in a storm.

Nature teaches us that the eye of a storm is usually to be found in the center of strong cyclones, and is approximately circular in shape and anywhere between twenty to forty miles in diameter. It is surrounded by something called an eye wall, which is the section where the storm is at its strongest.

Yet somewhat ironically, the lowest pressure of the storm is to be found in the eye itself. Basically the larger the eye, the less severe the storm is. The smaller the eye, the more severe the storm is. Furthermore, if the eye were to collapse completely, chaotic weather patterns would ensue and prevail.

Things had certainly changed in a moment for me. Until the dream I received about the murder, I did not see this coming. At some point after my brother's death, I had allowed myself to believe that maybe the stormy part of my life had subsided.

But this storm was so vicious in its wake, and dragged up everything that went before it as well. How could my father be scheming and manipulating the murder of my brother's wife on the day my brother was dying, knowing that he would create an orphan of their only son, let alone destroy the rest of the family? How could a father view his family as mere collateral damage in the pursuit of a relentless money seeking agenda?

Adversity often acts like a mirror, showing us the true substance within us, and these life events had come so thick and fast with very little recovery time. As I looked in the mirror of adversity, all I could see was an inner world that was collapsing fast.

How big was my inner 'eye' of the storm? Up till now, I had courage and determination, but essentially what little self-esteem I had was collapsing, and I sensed this was key to my 'inner eye'.

I felt like a boxer who had collapsed on the floor after receiving relentless punches while against the ropes. I did not know where to start to disentangle the additional and accumulating layers of health challenges and financial pressure. However, those layers seemed thin compared to the immediate crisis of wondering whether I would ever wake up happy to be alive again.

I sat alone in the dark. My eyes were so sore from lost sleep that they had become light sensitive, so I craved the dark. My head was pounding. Every external sound seemed amplified. My head was so full of the noise of the world, including residual noise from the past, like an inner tinnitus. I craved silence and became even more socially withdrawn.

The only thing that had been holding me up to now was the part of the dream that informed me that I would not be destroyed. Now it felt like this was no longer enough to hold me. I decided to shut off to my intuition, because all it seemed to be associated with was death and warnings. My eye of the storm was collapsing fast, and the radius did not feel that big to start with.

I had survived many blows in life. Would this be the final straw that defeated me and took me under? The horrible repercussions of not finding a foothold on life swirled round me with frightening pull and velocity.

I was at the mercy of the storm, and its message was that I needed to quickly rebuild the center piece that was my inner eye of the storm, or be utterly destroyed!

PART 2

THE PRISON

'Be thine own palace, or the world's thy jail'

John Donne

THE AWAKENING

THE MOST SIGNIFICANT CHANGES AND GROWTH IN MY LIFE HAVE STEMMED from an awakening or epiphany. This was no different.

As I viewed the landscape of my life, all I could see was the devastation left by the latest event. The dream I had as a child, of a close family that would be deeply loving and hospitable towards others, lay smashed to pieces. The dream I had of being married with children lay in tatters in the light of my sexuality.

The dream I had of making a difference as a humanitarian contributor was shattered as I felt broken, unable to function, and damaged beyond repair.

All I could see were the fragments of a former life, scattered in unrecognizable pieces. I felt hollowed out and empty. I could not feel my body, even though I could see it. Some part of me wanted to depart, and yet something kept me still.

I collapsed in a heap on the floor, alone in the dark and silence, too tired to feel much, yet too aware not to notice the disillusionment, anguish, guilt, resentment and shame that had been quietly gnawing away at my soul.

Over the next month, waves of intense mourning left my eyes feeling sore and swollen. They were followed by brief interludes of calm, which felt more like reprieve than resolution of grief. I sat for long periods staring ahead aimlessly, unable to coordinate thought or movement in more than a momentary fashion.

It is one thing to mourn when someone dies of illness in the family, but it is a completely different type of bereavement when one member of the family deliberately and willfully takes the life of another family member. That grief was immobilizing me.

To think that years ago I wanted to be a detective in the police force, but wasn't tall enough. Now I had solved my own family murder before the police. It all felt like a sick joke.

I was aware from my training in psychiatry about the different stages of grief – denial, bargaining, depression, anger, and acceptance.

However none of those stages of grief seemed apt in their description when, one day, in a moment of reprieve, I found myself strongly tempted to get a gun and put it to my father's head to inflict back on him the very pain he had delivered to my sister-in-law. A life sentence of fifteen years did not seem enough for what my father did. By the same token we had only been given a fifteen year reprieve from this behavior.

However revenge was not the enduring thought. My thoughts surpassed this state to a more practical consideration. What if I killed him before he could kill again? I could stop our lives from being defined by the anticipation of another murderous cycle reconvening, should he ever be released, which I was told was unlikely. After all, he had continued to maintain his innocence, and believed we had conspired to put him behind bars. He might seek revenge.

The incident regarding Mum's near collapse at work in October 1992 led me to believe that Dad's murderous intent would have continued had he not been arrested. Who knows what other measures he would have taken to wipe out the family, in order to get his hands on any potential source of money?

Would Dad now play the criminal system in order to secure potential release? Would he maintain good behavior for fifteen years, even if he felt no remorse?

The police seemed to think that he would not have the physical frame to commit murder if he ever came out. How they missed the point!

They did not seem to want to accommodate that at fifty five years old psychology had played the upper hand in the execution of his planned murder, not his physique.

I felt quite calm, lucid and rational at this point. They say revenge is best served cold. Had the focus of my thoughts taken me to this calm but cold place? The idea of putting a revolver to my father's head seemed to hang suspended in time, long after the original thought emerged.

Then, as if woken suddenly from an altered state of consciousness, a fresh wave of horror took over me. What was I becoming in all this, that I could entertain such foreign thoughts to my own character? Was I just like my father? We had often been compared as alike in personality – charming, strong willed, strong minded and stubborn.

Was I now just absorbing and taking on his thoughts, by wanting to end his life? I wanted to get out of my skin, and cleanse myself. It took conscious thought and effort to prize myself away from that notion, and tell myself that whilst we might be alike in some aspects of our personalities, we stood for different values.

Then I had an awakening moment, an epiphany, as a picture emerged before me. It was to complete a turning point in my quest to recover and find life again. That turning point had been signaled initially by the dream in the night which foretold this latest life event.

It came round full circle as I pondered my father's imprisonment, because what got reflected back in my mind's eye was an image of me behind prison bars. My father was in a physical prison with bars made of steel which prevented his freedom from the outside world.

I was in the outside world, supposedly free, yet living within an inner prison. My bars were made of bitterness, hate, anger, resentment, vindictiveness, blame, disillusionment, self- loathing, fear and distrust.

Unless I found the key to break free from this inner prison, I was as good as in a physical cell, next to my father. I felt like the walking dead. I had a decision to make – to release the true person I was and discover life, or become a prisoner to my past, and merely exist at best as a recovered victim.

Spurned by the shock and realization of this picture, I decided in that moment that I would make this journey. That decision was made more out of fear and desperation than desire, but it was a start.

The deep understanding of human nature acquired from my life experience and work in psychiatry combined, had helped me uncover the murder. I suspected this would not be enough for the journey I now needed to make.

It is interesting, that for all the knowledge I gained from psychiatry alone, we were not taught transformational skills. Psychiatry had equipped me with self-awareness skills, management and functional skills, and that would have to be my starting point. I deposited this decision into my 'eye of the storm'. I had no idea how I would find the other resources or answers, but I knew that the dream I had foretelling the disaster held further clues.

There is a difference between what I call head knowledge and heart knowledge. For me an epiphany or awakening bypasses the conscious mind, and involves the heart and intuition. It touches every cell within with a knowledge and certainty that the head alone doesn't give. The prison cell image had awoken me to a fresh perspective that gave me crucial insight about the journey ahead.

My cells needed more of these insights and awakenings if I was to survive, let alone live. It was time to revisit the dream which led to revealing the murder, but for very different reasons.

THE TURNING POINT

THE CATALYST

IT SEEMS STRANGE THAT THE PAIN OF ADVERSITY IS OFTEN THE VEHICLE and catalyst for massive change for so many people. My situation was no different in this respect. However, although many were applauding me for being one of life's survivors, it started to ring hollow.

I might have looked well-adjusted and together on the outside but I was barely surviving. I was grateful to have survived the latest adversity. I was relieved to be able to regain functionality to cope with daily routines again, as part of tending to my basic human existence. However, as I started to consider a long term future I wanted to feel more. I wanted to feel alive on the inside again.

The hunger and desire for more was an encouraging sign that healing was taking place. I knew I had to continue with the process of healing in order for that feeling of life to come through more strongly, and there was still so much surrounding past adversity to process.

The layers of adversity for me were multiple – some were circumstantial and others came from within. For example, the stigmatizing effects of the murder ran deep as some sections of society blamed my family for what happened. They applied the 'guilty by association' label to us and effectively treated us like criminals. We were subjected to public outbursts of anger.

Others viewed us through 'medical eyes', by seeing every vulnerable expression as being dysfunctional and part of a depressive illness. As far as the inner layers of adversity were concerned, I knew I had to go back to the dream as my starting point, because it revealed far more than just an event. The dream held clues for the journey I was about to embark on, and I needed to decode it further.

The Dream 1992

In the dream I found myself in an autumn scene in a field of hay where the bales were ready for harvest. This was usually one of my favorite reflective spots.

However, in this dream my heart was so full of grief that it felt like I was carrying physical weight far too heavy to bear. I staggered under the weight. A close friend of mine was trying to reach out and comfort me, but I shunned her away as I wanted to be alone. She walked off with sadness in her eyes.

I collapsed from the weight of my grief behind a bale of hay, lay face down, and sobbed for ages. As I lifted my head momentarily, out of the corner of my left eye I could see a lion. I did not know where it came from, and at that moment I resigned myself to the fact that I was going to be eaten alive. I had no fight left.

To my surprise the lion came and sat down beside me and put its paw around me. As I lifted my head more, I noticed that there was a little child under me of no more than three years of age. I was amazed that I had not noticed her. She looked like me when I was three years old. She appeared vulnerable and was looking intently into my eyes for support. I was in disbelief that I did not feel her physical frame under my body.

As I looked up, I noticed a man setting the field alight with a match in the far right corner of the field. I turned to the lion and said 'surely he is not going to destroy the only place that means anything to me, where I feel safe'. Before I knew it the whole field was ablaze.

The lion pulled me up with the toddler, and we seemed to fly to a place where there was a stream at the bottom end of the field behind me. The lion placed us down just as the fire reached the verge, and disappeared. The man who had set fire to the field had gone too. For what seemed ages, I stood with this toddler in my arms, looking on at the devastation of a burnt field, yet also wondered in amazement about the great rescue by the lion and its significance.

Dream ends…

Dream Interpretation

'And the end of all our exploring will be to arrive where we started and know the place for the first time'

TS Eliot

The dream took place in one of my favorite seasons and reflective spots – the autumn harvest fields where hay is baled. I used to sit on a bale of hay in the autumn and play my guitar. I loved the autumn colors. I loved watching the tractors gather the harvest. I associated autumn with reaping the fruits of labor, and new beginnings. It would usually represent a time of mild evaluation, rest and creative planning. Not on this occasion.

This scene in this dream symbolized the robbery of all things good in my life at the hands of my father.

The intense grief I felt was an accumulation of the unresolved painful emotions arising from my family experiences, my identity and sexuality, now too heavy to hide. It was also an anticipated grief that came from knowing that more adversity was around the corner.

I was watching someone who had been drained of life, and now felt destroyed to the point of no return. I had coped with my painful emotions by suppressing them, and the dream was showing me that I would no longer be able to do this.

The close friend in my dream was from my nursing course, and the dream exposed how afraid I was to be vulnerable and show emotion in front of her and others. I was afraid to let anyone near me. I was afraid to trust.

I felt like a little lion cub, once courageous, that had had to grow into a lion too soon. I had been provoked and assaulted once too much, I could barely walk, let alone run. I had 'bandages' over inner wounds yet to heal, and I was scared to let anyone see or remove them.

So I pushed people away who came close to me – better to reject before I got rejected further. In the dream, when I fell and collapsed from the weight of my grief behind a bale of hay, this depicted the weight of unresolved grief which made my body feel very heavy. It also revealed my tendency to hide painful emotion from others, and mourn privately out of sight.

The lion represented God in the dream. You may know God as Universal Power or Intelligence, or by some other name. You may not believe in God. It does not matter. The fact that I thought I was going to be eaten alive by the lion very much represented my fear of God's impending wrath and punishment over my sexuality. The dream revealed my perception to be erroneous.

I was running but could not hide from God. God saw my situation and pain. So when the lion put its paw around me, the message was that God was very much by my side and there to help me. I was as shocked by this as I was at the scene that was playing out before me.

As for only noticing the child that lay beneath me on the ground, it was only when the lion put its paw around me, symbolizing safety and protection, that I then saw the little child. The lion's paw represented the safe and protective environment which encouraged the child to make herself visible.

That little child was me, afraid and in need of protection, yet increasingly dismissed and suppressed in childhood, as I had to grow up fast. The child's innocent and vulnerable expression was a communication of the unmet need for acknowledgment, safety and nurturance that persisted into adulthood.

In the dream I could barely make out the figure of a man in the corner of the field, yet somehow I knew it was my father. The setting of the field on fire was symbolic of the nature of the destructive adversity that was about to take place quickly at his hands.

However, as much as the dream foretold devastation it also informed me that a subtext or bigger theme was playing out, as portrayed by the lion grabbing me and the toddler, and flying us swiftly to a place of safety where the fire could not burn us.

I knew from this that although I would feel destroyed, I would not be destroyed, and that though my own human strength would feel insufficient, God's grace would carry me and plug the gap. It alluded to an inspirational journey of love and self-reconciliation in the aftermath.

What was powerful about this dream was not just what it foretold by way of event, but also the multi-dimensional psychological and inner profile it revealed about me. This dream confirmed that there was an outer and inner layer to my challenges.

The outer layer represented the circumstances that had played out and those yet to befall. The inner layer represented the various aspects of the relationship with myself, informed by the experiences of my upbringing.

The message was that this relationship portrayed emotional poverty. The lack of real bonding and deep connection was stopping me from feeling alive and free. It was a form of imprisonment, where I was chained to a past of unresolved conflicts and emotions. The power of the prison analogy was not lost on me.

It was spot on and no text book could have awakened me to my inner profile so accurately in a way that registered at cell level, not just head level.

'Adversity holds subtext for growth and vision'

A Narayan

I was starting to get a stronger glimpse of the message from the dream, that adversity holds subtext for growth and vision. A subtext is a message that points to a bigger theme than the apparent message.

It was hard to grasp in reality, but I knew that the promise of restoration from the dream was to become one of several anchors I put down, to keep me as centered as possible for the journey I was about to undergo. Here are some of the things I identified as part of my self- imprisonment, which I refer to as prison bars, along with the anchors I put down to get a foothold on my life.

Prison Bars and Anchors

My Prison Bars

Let's suppose I invited you for a meal at my home and you had never been here before. You get lost en route and then ring me to say so. What is the first question I am going to ask you?

'Where are you?'

Only then can I redirect you from where you are to my place. It would be hard to do so if you told me you were somewhere else when you were not there at all. Dishonesty and denial are like being in that place and it is difficult to move with direction, purpose or accuracy from a place of deception or denial.

I knew I had to acknowledge the nature of my prison bars with honesty if I was to gain any sort of movement and momentum on this journey.

Prison Bar 1 – Fear

I was afraid that I would never be able to wake up and feel happy to be alive again. I was fearful that I would never find romantic feelings for men ever again and was haunted by my feelings towards women. The thought of trusting another human being again made me afraid. The experience of emotions such as rage filled me with terror. I was scared to let others see my vulnerability and I was petrified of intimacy. I was afraid I would never be able to forgive my father. Even more, I dreaded the thought of not being able to break free from my inner prison.

PRISON BAR 2 – BITTERNESS

I felt bitterness towards my father for all the pain and suffering he had inflicted on the family, for rendering my nephew an orphan, for the damage he inflicted on my Mum and sister, for the financial debt I accrued for the first time in my life as a result of the ongoing trial.

In a strange way I felt bitter toward my Mum for blaming me for the first divorce, for not offering me enough protection, for showing divided loyalty, for the role reversal that played out as a child where I was more the parent than the child.

I also resented God – why give me the dream after the event when I couldn't save my sister-in-law? Why not be spiritually guided before my brother died, so I could help him? It was all too much, and God's timing seemed to be way out, or maybe I was way out of tune. So my bitterness turned inward too.

My bitterness was also directed towards the church. Their answer to my sexuality when I eventually found the courage to share my torment was to cast demons out and consign me to a life of celibacy. That in itself was like being given a prison sentence.

They also believed if you did not tithe your money and give it to the church, you would not be blessed in your life. Why should I tithe and be obliged to give my money to the church? Why could I not give my money freely to causes without applying a rigid formula and rule, or have others control my choice? The bitterness was often accompanied by anger.

PRISON BAR 3 – SELF HATE

This was like anger turned inwards. I hated myself for my changing sexual orientation, and I was aware I had not really addressed this because of other more immediate and heavy duty events. I was full of self-loathing for not being able to feel any deep intimacy towards men beyond affection.

I was full of self-hate for not being able to save my brother and my sister-in-law. I detested myself for being so outspoken and courageous. Maybe if I had kept my mouth shut at eleven years old, things would have turned out differently.

Prison Bar 4 – Guilt/Shame

I felt ashamed about the family events that had unfolded, ashamed of my changing sexuality because the church considered it immoral. On top of the self-hate, I felt guilty and responsible for the deaths of my brother and sister-in-law.

I should have been stronger and stayed at home longer and maybe my brother would still be alive. If I hadn't gone to London after my brother had died maybe I would have noticed the chain of events leading to the murder of my sister-in-law, and somehow prevented it.

Prison Bar 5 – Depression

My depression went deep. My voice was monotone, and my body felt heavy even though I was losing weight fast. My mantra was 'death would be a sweet release'. The desire to die without acting on those feelings is often referred to by psychiatrists as passive suicide. It was hard enough to get through the day, and I was socially withdrawn because I did not like my own company, let alone inflict my miserable self on others.

I did not want others to see how bad I felt. Counselling sucked. Was it me, the counsellor or the process? I don't know. I just never felt any progress. It took energy to keep talking too, so I stopped after a while. I could not imagine waking up and feeling happy to be alive. I could not see a future.

Prison Bar 6 – Rigid Thinking

I was aware that I had this 'black and white' thinking. Things were either right or wrong, they were this or that. There was nothing in between. For a long time this thinking had given me a sense of security, and now I realized it gave me a false sense of security because its answers were inadequate for my current situation and did not address the uncertainty I felt.

I had bowed to the conditioning of my upbringing, and had adopted the teachings of the church without really owning those beliefs for myself. To question the conditioned thinking left me questioning who I really was. Was I the sum total of adopted teachings or was there anything I owned? I was confused.

So I looked my prison bars straight in the face. I knew I had to acknowledge them before I could move on. It was painful to observe and acknowledge. So I sat and acknowledged my pain too.

I knew that any change could bring about uncertainty and anxiety, so I needed to draw on strengths that would act like anchors and create some stability for the inner journey ahead.

Anchor 1: Courage

Courage seemed to be a gift I possessed since childhood. So far it had turned out to be a double edged sword, which had nearly cost me my life at the hands of my father. Still, although I felt out of courage, I was going to need this in greater measure for the journey ahead.

I never seemed to hesitate to speak out against injustice, and this was to get cultivated further when I went on to work for the Royal College of Nursing in my next career, which I talk about shortly. Part of that job was to represent nurses in industrial relations cases. There were some ugly cases too. For example, I would be party to cases where nurses would be disciplined on issues they were completely unaware of, without the manager scrutinizing their own neglect in communicating concerns along the way. Some cases would have validity, but many were rooted in prejudice, which resulted in bullying and discrimination.

Bravery would be needed to help with the upbringing of my young nephew. It would also be needed to counter the waves of public humility my family had to go through as a result of twisted media reporting. However, the greatest courage would be needed in my own recovery, especially in facing the inner conflicts of self-esteem and identity.

ANCHOR 2: FUN AND HUMOR

First of all, I decided to keep a picture of myself as a three year old on my desk wall, where I would see it every day, to remind me of my true personality – as a toddler I was known for my infectious laughter, and this was noted by my primary school teachers when I started school.

I also had a rather cheeky sense of humor that followed me through childhood to adulthood. I believe that my sense of humor saved my life in the true sense of the word. Right now I couldn't laugh or see the funny side of things any more. I was going to have to rediscover that. Here is the picture I kept in front of me.

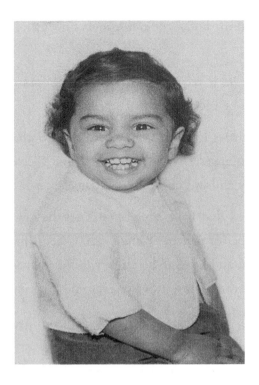

What a little poser I was!! Moving on swiftly…

ANCHOR 3: FOOTBALL

I decided to start playing competitive football again. I had originally started to play competitively in the women's league and for the region when I was twenty six years old. I stopped for three years when I commenced my nurse training in 1990, due to shift work.

Football has always been the one activity where I have felt a sense of freedom as a player. As a child I had to play behind my parent's back, now I could play with complete abandon and freedom.

Right now football was to play an even bigger therapeutic role, in helping me to break the feeling of detachment from the world. I broke into the first team very quickly, and so the physical intensity of playing football mobilized my body, got endorphins flowing, and provided some emotional release.

At a deeper level it reconnected me to life because it also kept me connected to a game I loved and had a passion for.

During my thirties I played some of my best football, in spite of the traumatic circumstances I was processing. I got selected for the region again very quickly and was chosen to captain the team later.

Again, I learned that I was able to channel the raw emotion of pain into exceptional performances on the pitch. Often I picked up player of the match awards, and I was to go on to win the 'manager's player of the season' trophy for three consecutive years, something that no other player in the team had achieved.

ANCHOR 4: HELPING OTHERS

Across my life it had always been my prayer to maintain capacity to be there for others, no matter how bad things got with life in general. It was an enduring value.

Since childhood, I had developed a reputation for helping others no matter what was going on for me. This ability and capacity to look outside of myself was something I needed and wanted to maintain, not only to survive, but to keep some sense of self. The nature of nursing gave me that opportunity further.

The person that needed my help most of all right now would be my nephew. He was only two years old when he was orphaned, and nine years old when Dad was put in prison. The next ten years were to be devoted to helping my Mum and sister with his upbringing, when I was not at work.

ANCHOR 5: NATURE

Nature has always been a powerful mix of awesome beauty and an amazing teacher of life lessons for me. I recall reading about the oyster and how pearls are formed.

Contrary to popular belief, a pearl is not formed by a grain of sand. Natural pearls are created by oysters, known as bivalves. This means that their shell is made of two parts of valve. The shell's valves are held together by an elastic ligament, and this ligament is positioned where the valves come together. It usually keeps the valves open so the oyster can eat.

As the oyster grows in size its shell must also grow. The mantle is an organ that produces the oyster's shell using minerals from the oyster's food. The material created by the mantle is called nacre.

The formation of natural pearls takes place when a foreign substance such as a parasite enters between the mantle and the shell. The parasite will then worm its way and irritate the mantle tissue of the oyster.

This effect will cause the epithelial cells to form a sac around the parasite or intruder, and then deposit a calcium carbonate substance known as nacre, which is the building block of pearls. Layers of nacre formed around the irritant eventually produce the pearl.

Who would believe that the oyster could turn an irritant into something of miraculous value, as it secretes nacre to protect itself?

What a wonderful analogy for life transformation and miracles - to be able to take current reality, use a creative power from within, and transform that into something of value thereby creating a completely different reality.

An irritant was something of an understatement for the circumstance I faced. Still, I understood in essence that I was going to learn to develop the capacity to bring good out of this challenge, and to channel the pain of the 'cards' life had dealt me, into something of great value.

FINDING THE CODE

The next ten months were particularly challenging, because it took a long time for my thyroid to level out. Sixteen weeks of non-treatment as a result of not being informed about my medical diagnosis had created a huge energy deficit. In fact it was to take nearly a year of thyroid treatment before I started to feel any sort of equilibrium again. In the meantime my energy had changed from free flowing to sluggish in the first couple of hours in the morning.

During this period of my life my main focus was my nephew and his care. I didn't let him see what was really going on inside of me. I had to be strong for him, and he was a pleasure to bring up. When alone, I just crumbled in a heap and slept a lot. I slept heavily, yet I never felt rested. Most days I just felt disorientated, as if gripped by an inner concussion.

These months were all about resurfacing and learning to get through the day. It was hard to distract myself for any length of time from the awareness of what had happened with my father. I still could not grasp or fathom the whole thing, and the event constantly played out like a dull ache and inner echo in my head.

For many days I just sat in silence, staring ahead, swinging between taking in the reality of what had gone before, and feeling vacant and empty.

What energy I had was directed toward my nephew and family, to try and support and impart some comfort and strength in this recovery phase, yet I felt so inadequate.

It did not stop me offering support as I decided not to let it get in the way. However it made me more aware of the need to get help for myself in order to strengthen the base of that support. The complex issues around a murder within the family meant that I was on new ground where recovery was concerned, so I could not draw solely on other past experiences of healing from grief.

In the early days of recovery sleep was a huge healing mechanism. In the autumn I decided to re-engage in competitive football with my local club in Basingstoke.

Slowly, I regained some sense of footing on the ladder of survival. In January 1996, some eight months after my time out, I woke up one morning feeling alert as if some life was returning to my system.

This alertness continued for several days, and for the first time I considered returning to work in some form. I felt stuck on this matter though because the rent for my flat was double the amount of my previous place, even though it was a council flat.

I needed to earn double my nursing salary so that I could come off medical government benefits. Now usually I would have prayed about that, but at this point I was still conditioned by the belief that my relationship with God had been cut following my departure from the church. Prayer seemed an invalid option in light of my lack of confidence.

So what I did was to simply ask the question out loud, to no-one in particular, as to how I could earn double my previous salary within the nursing sector. I did not realize the power of what I was doing at that moment, and I shall return to this point in part three of this book. For now, it was an instinctive thing.

Within three weeks the answer appeared in miraculous fashion. No-one had been party to any conversation about my decision to seek work again. After three weeks I got a call from the local regional office of The Royal College of Nursing.

The Royal College of Nursing is the nurse's professional, educational and industrial relations organization, and the role of an officer was to work alongside nurses in those three areas. I had worked on a three month secondment for them in 1995, and had made a hugely positive impression during that time.

A secondment is a loan period of work with another employer for a predetermined spell in order to gain work experience and skills that will be mutually beneficial. I would remain under contract to my local mental health hospital for the purpose of pay and related entitlements.

I did have opportunity to apply for a permanent role there beyond my secondment, but I made a mess of the interview and was unsuccessful, because my answers to the interview questions were too short, according to the panel.

The reason I gave inadequate answers was because the panel was formed of key staff from my secondment. They had seen my performance first hand. Therefore I assumed it was not necessary to expand on my answers too much. That assumption cost me the interview.

This call I received in January 1996 was from the same office asking me to call the manager of another regional office in Banbury, Oxfordshire. They were seeking someone on a temporary basis to cover sick leave or maternity leave, and this manager wanted to talk to me.

I did not know this person or any other office beyond my region, but went along to meet her in Banbury. I remember feeling a mixture of curiosity, excitement and fear. How was I going to explain my current situation and convince anyone that they should employ me, when I could just about function to make it through the day, doing very little?

I knew how involved and stretching this career would be from the experience of my secondment. It certainly wasn't a step down from nursing, just different in the way it employed certain skill sets on a much wider platform.

What happened next showed me the better side of human nature. When I met the manager in Banbury, I had already decided I would give full disclosure about my circumstances and my general current state, so that whatever happened came from a place of honesty and informed decision making.

I don't know what I expected, but this manager insisted on employing me at full salary, and the salary was to be double what I had earned in nursing, which would enable me to pay my rent. Amazing!

I even tried to argue against this, due to the worry I had about my current level of functioning and application, but I was encouraged not to be anxious. They believed in me and would give me all the support I needed.

I cried as I drove home. I was not used to such kindness and support, and had learned not to expect it. As strange as it felt, it was so lovely to experience this side of human nature. Maybe God had not abandoned me? Whatever the case, this was certainly another one of those 'happenings' where I was being looked after in spite of my lack of faith.

It's interesting how when we are inwardly ready for change, providence turns up. I had no idea that anyone knew me from the further reaches of upper Oxford, but my reputation had reportedly spread from the days when I won a landmark student case during my nurse training. The subsequent secondment to the local office had only enhanced my reputation.

It was encouraging for me to have this experience of people spreading positive endorsement, and was in stark contrast to my experience with the media throughout the murder investigation and trial.

I was not prepared for just how hard it would be to work again. I nearly resigned in the first week as I found it hard to coordinate my thoughts and focus. Simple tasks like photocopying and writing a standard letter seemed to take extra coordination of thought.

It was such a long way to fall after exhibiting such a high minimum baseline of functioning. However I had a very caring boss who saw past this, and was able to hold perspective for me where I had lost it.

That nurturing approach was responsible for helping me to find my feet, and for my success in starting some innovative projects in nursing. I eventually took on a full time post in London.

I am grateful to my former boss to this day, for showing me this patient, compassionate and caring side of human nature, and for believing in my gifts and talents in spite of the traumatic effect of my circumstances. The same applies to my first manager in nursing. This was a departure from how the majority were viewing me.

The attribute of being bold, along with my analytical ability and articulation in the face of injustice, won me many an industrial relations case for nurses. I learned that a strong sense of justice was not a bad trait, even if it came with a price that required much sustained courage.

My nephew was in boarding school in the next county during my five year tenure at The Royal College of Nursing, so it was easier to access him and provide support. My sister was also in the neighboring county, so we were able to share the responsibility between us.

The outlet of assisting others through my work got me back in touch with that part of myself that loved helping others. However, when I was alone I wrestled with patches of detachment and depression, and still felt empty.

There were many residual issues from the trial to deal with, and we also had the challenge of seeing Mum almost die from cancer. A lifesaving operation on a malignant ovarian cyst prevented her from dying. I seemed to take that in my stride quite calmly. I am not sure if that was because the traumatic circumstances of the past had toughened me, or because I had detached from my feelings in order to cope and function.

Personally I think both were true. I was still feeling detached from the world in 1997, two years after my father's imprisonment. So I decided to go to Canada for two weeks that autumn and stay in a log cabin near the lakes, trees and mountains.

The log cabin was in the grounds of a forest. The only thing I had to contend with was the testosterone driven elk, but I think they knew instinctively to give me room and space, rather than charge at me with their horns!

The combination of fresh clean air, sun, trees, mountains and lakes, along with staying in a log cabin parked in a nature reserve, proved medicinal for me. More importantly it got me reconnected with life. I felt earthed again, and it was a relief. Nature had come to the rescue. My detachment was dissolving and I was starting to 'feel' again.

The moderate depression started to break up, a bit like the clouds breaking to give way to blue sky and sunshine. I did not feel in the clear yet, but at least there was movement.

It was about this time that I had my first relationship with a woman. I was thirty five years old. She lived close by so we had interacted with each other for some months as neighbors. We grew closer over that time and on her initiation we engaged in a relationship. I let her know how nervous I was because this was my first relationship with a woman, and she seemed to respond in a very caring and patient manner. However within a couple of weeks of this new relationship, jealousy and possessiveness came to the fore in her behavior.

She was not working and I was. Each day when I returned from work, she became demanding of immediate attention emotionally and sexually. When I could not just switch on to her sexual demands, she resorted to physical aggression and accused me of unfaithfulness.

Any feelings of love and intimacy I had originally experienced got suffocated in the presence of her behavior, and I decided I needed to get out of the relationship after several months. I was quite shocked to see a woman behaving with such aggression.

When I tried to get out of the relationship she was not accepting of my decision and would not leave me alone for a long time. I felt like I was being stalked at times and due to the close vicinity in which we lived it was hard to get any distance from this. Eventually, she then left the neighborhood, much to my relief

My first relationship with a woman had turned out to be the worst I ever had. I did not want to be on the receiving end of possessive and violent behavior especially when I did not treat others like this. I certainly did not wish to be reminded of my Dad's behavior either. It was the first time I experienced that women could be violent, and this shocked me. Was I just too naive? I felt drained.

My second relationship was not initiated by me either. In fact I rarely initiated a relationship, mainly because I was very unassuming and naïve when it came to knowing whether a person was attracted to me and I feared rejection.

This relationship was better. However it ended after a few months because I could not accept a lifestyle where I kept the company of women only, and avoided socializing with men. This was the lifestyle my second partner wanted for me and I did not want to fit into that constraint.

For all I had been through, I did not hate men, and wanted a healthy mix of friends, irrespective of gender or other labels. So this relationship also ended. It was a bit of a shock to see women behaving in such a possessive and constraining way.

I stayed on my own for a few years after that, and pretty much felt asexual for most of the time.

I loved my work with the Royal College of Nursing, but it was intensive and made more so by my desire to give one hundred per-cent, so I was drained by the end of the day. London had a very transient population and came with its own challenges. That, coupled with increasing amounts of industrial relations cases, was squashing the amount of time left to do other more proactive work.

Unable to regenerate properly, in spite of playing football, my energy started to suffer, and my thyroid needed increased medication to hold it over the following months. There were still residual issues from the trial, and I started to struggle with low mood and depression again.

One day I paced my lounge and somewhere from deep within I stated 'that's enough, I am fed up with feeling depressed. I have to find the code to change this!'

In the beginning of this episode there was a sense in which the depression protected me because my system shut down as if in overwhelm. Every day felt black even if there was something to feel good about. That made every day predictable. I knew that if I did not break free I would remain with a false sense of security, and stuck in depression.

'When the student is ready the teacher appears'

Chinese proverb

While the need to feel secure is a basic human need, the need to feel safe and secure was even stronger right now for me, but I did not want that need to be fed by depression. I decided I was not going to take any more anti-depressant medication, as it just had a numbing and dumbing effect on me.

I had no clue how I was going to break free from depression, but just knew I would by the nature of the decision I made. As the Chinese proverb goes 'when the student is ready the teacher appears'

I sat down one day in quiet contemplation and reflected on how I felt about my life and my work. I recalled how, many years ago, I had harbored dreams of having a loving marriage and family, and doing something entrepreneurial which would allow me to contribute to humanitarian causes in a big way.

My attempts to explore my sexuality had resulted in two unfulfilling relationships, and the concept of creating a loving family seemed long dead. However the seeds of humanitarianism had been sown through nursing. The entrepreneurial dream, though distant, was at least something with a slim possibility.

The experience with The Royal College of Nursing had highlighted certain ingredients that I wanted to carry over into any entrepreneurial journey – the autonomy to work on my own with my own geographical patch, yet within a team environment and expression. I loved the combination of autonomy, operational freedom, and expression through a collaborative team approach.

It allowed me to develop and express my gifts, yet have greater impact through collective expression. During my five year career with the Royal College of Nursing, I had started to explore the entrepreneurial route by starting a small business with nutritional supplements in the health niche.

This was a natural extension of my taking natural products that had helped with depression. I had a degree of success on a small scale, given the little time I had to run the business.

The other thing that occurred to me, reflecting back on the dream I had, was that it was not enough to simply free myself from the depression that had set in. I also needed to find some sort of life purpose again. Right now I just felt like a recovering victim who had found some resources to keep intact through work and daily existence.

However, outside of that, I felt empty and lost on a personal level. The skills I had learnt in psychiatry along with my life experiences, had bought me so far. I needed something different and something more.

I would try anything, even if I had to suspend my understanding of any process for now. I got introduced to neuro-linguistic programming by a close friend. This helped me achieve some sense of progress on the issue of depression by helping me see how I was processing things, and how I could create new associations with health.

I remembered that I used to meditate and I tried to start it again, but my concentration was so poor, I could not maintain it. I also craved silence. For some reason since the murder, I had become quite noise sensitive, and silence provided some antidote to this.

The pull to run my own business continued to grow, so one day I sat down and reflected on what I thought would be the best expression of my gifts within a business context. Something in me knew that the answer was in my life journey, and as I reflected back, I remembered how I had naturally put winning sports teams together at middle school.

Perhaps the defining moment was the memory of my Physical Education teacher's end of term report at upper school. She was a disciplinarian by nature, which made the report I received from her that much more meaningful.

In that report she said that I was the best pupil she had ever had the pleasure to teach, and not simply because I was outstanding in sports performance, but because I was always humble about it and willing to help others with their sports development.

So this was how I came to identify coaching as the natural extension of a gift into the business arena.

I completed my first Football Coaching Certificate out of my love for football. I then embarked on my life coaching certificate in 2000, and shortly afterwards attended a Tony Robbins weekend. Amongst other things, I had my first experience of walking on twelve foot of hot coals. As new as this was, I realized I was a physical type of learner, and so I was naturally intrigued, and a bit scared.

This was the start of my first real breakthrough in recovery, because the symbolism I attached to the physical feat of walking across twelve foot of hot coals was 'I can'. I completed the task with only two hours training, and without burning my feet.

If you had asked me whether I thought it would be possible for me to walk across hot coals without getting burned, and with only two hours training, I would have replied 'impossible'. Yet here I was, demonstrating and making possible what I thought was impossible.

What was powerful about the experience was the demonstration to me that humans are capable of learning faster than they think. Also the very physical and emotional nature of this learning meant it would be difficult for me to hold the belief 'I can't', when I had just walked over coals with a combined temperature of several ovens put together! An old belief had now collapsed with an empowering new belief emerging.

I started to feel fresh hope again. I attended the Tony Robbins Mastery

University, a six month intensive course. It left me exhausted for several months afterwards, due to the intensive immersion type learning, coupled with my own energy status as my recovery continued.

Still, I took something important from that course when I did the forty foot fire walk. This became my symbol and metaphor, which took me beyond knowing 'I can', to knowing that 'I can make change last'. I carried out the forty foot coal walk successfully.

I now had two live symbolic anchors from which to address my two strongest fears, namely whether I could get through this trauma and make any change last. It was to take much time for these things to root properly, but it was a beginning. I found it inspirational.

It occurred to me that I needed more inspiration rather than mere education, to breathe fresh life into me. I needed to read true accounts of people who had overcome in areas where I felt stuck, such as forgiveness, fear, extreme adversity, and self-esteem. I needed to build on the theme of 'I can'.

The account of Roger Bannister was an inspiration to me, because he set out to break the four minute mile by shaving milliseconds off from his personal best on a regular basis. When he eventually broke the four minute mile, many went on to do so.

He had made the impossible possible by expanding his personal best. I learned from this that if one man can do it, it can be done. The experience with hot coals had given me my first real sense of ownership – the belief that I was able and capable of achieving dreams, and a life beyond mere survival.

The story of Bruce Lee was also inspirational for me. During his short time on earth he had a vision to spread the teachings of Kung Fu to all in the USA, irrespective of culture. He then hit a pivotal moment in his life. Certain factions of his culture became violently opposed to his teachings. One day he was left almost paralyzed as a result of an unlawful attack from behind by an adversary. He came to a 'make or break' point in his life.

Had he given up at that point, the book he wrote about Kung Fu would never have materialized or developed into a film. Instead he went within, took the inner lessons of Kung Fu which he had practiced and taught, and applied them to his own healing challenge. He effectively learned to create 'pearls' and used his inner resources to heal and write, with the help of his wife.

Something much bigger came out of his adversity which allowed his vision and message to expand in a bigger way than before. He had managed to transfer learning in one aspect of his life, and apply it to overcome a challenge in another area.

I started to scan areas of my life that had similar displays of strength I could draw on. For me it was my playing career in women's football. Football was the one activity where I felt complete freedom when I played. It was also a physical contact sport.

I knew that within the rules of the game of football, I might get tackled legitimately and fall over, or I might get fouled accidentally or deliberately.

'Challenges are a part of life rather than an intrusion on life'

A Narayan

I never stayed down or refused to get up, because it was part of the game, and the bigger focus was on scoring and defeating the opposition.

I knew that I needed to transfer that analogy to my life. I needed to change my perspective on life and accept that, like football, life is like a physical contact sport. Challenges are a part of life rather than an intrusion on life.

Although I was no longer attending church, the Biblical account of Joseph had held strong resonance for me since childhood because it had so many parallels to my life. Now it came back to echo in my situation. What particularly fascinated me was how Joseph found a new context for his life beyond his immediate suffering. How I needed to be able to do that!

Joseph was a man of many dreams, who lived in Israel. One day, out of jealousy, his brothers threw him into a pit and left him for dead. Some travelling Egyptians caught sight of Joseph, took him to Egypt, and sold him as a slave to King Pharaoh.

Far from home and his dream, his plight worsened when he was wrongly accused of making a pass at Pharaoh's daughter, and he ended up in prison. At that point he could not have been further from his dreams.

He ended up interpreting the dreams of two of his inmates with accuracy, and word of this spread. One day he was called to interpret some dreams that were troubling Pharaoh, in which he predicted a seven year famine would take place, after seven years of abundance in the land.

Literally overnight, he was promoted to the second most important man in the land, second only to Pharaoh. As governor, he orchestrated the saving of grain in the time of abundance so that the Egyptians would be provided for when the famine struck.

When it did, his brothers ended up travelling to Egypt for provision of food. When they realized it was Joseph heading up the provision, they were overcome with remorse for the way they had treated him. Likewise,

Joseph was overcome with emotion, but not in the way many would predict.

This was captured in his response to his brothers' remorse, when he responded by saying,

'And now do not be distressed and do not be angry with yourselves for selling me here, because it was to save lives that God sent me ahead of you.' [Genesis 45 v5]

'You intended to harm me but God intended it for good to accomplish what is now being done, the saving of many lives' [Genesis 50 v20]

This was an account of broken dreams, jealous rage, attempted murder, injustice, but ultimately an account in which a bigger picture unfolded, a picture that resulted in gracious provision, insight, remorse, forgiveness, compassion and reconciliation.

One theme the above had in common was how they saw opportunity in adversity, developed a higher purpose, and turned things round, according to the vision that developed.

Like Joseph, I had experienced dreams. Similarly it had caused jealousy or threat in others. As with Joseph, I was the subject of murderous intent, had left my hometown and served out different jobs. Similarly to Joseph, I had experienced wrong accusation, and ended up in prison, though mine was an inner prison.

I knew that I needed a different perspective of my adversity if things were to change outwardly, so for now I just asked out of curiosity 'what if there is a bigger picture to all that has happened to me in this adversity?'

I needed to have a new context for my life, beyond that of recovering victim, which would allow some sense of life purpose to find expression.

I decided to entertain that thought and just hold on to it in spite of my immediate feelings. For now I could only sense a bigger purpose in my life. I could not experience it in any real tangible way as yet.

Nelson Mandela's account of finding freedom during physical imprisonment also spurred me on. I was starting to grasp that the key to my inner freedom lay within me.

The final account that inspired me was Desmond Tutu's story of ending apartheid in South Africa. I had always marveled at how Desmond Tutu exuded this effervescent joy in the face of such darkness, and it gave me a glimpse of the concept that joy was something separate to circumstance, and accessible from within.

However, where this book really helped me break through was in the area of forgiveness. Up until this point I struggled badly with the idea of forgiving my father. I still held him responsible for my brother's death indirectly, in addition to the murder.

When I read his account, I was astounded at the magnanimity of the women and families who agreed to an amnesty, which Desmond Tutu proposed and facilitated. These families had been dehumanized, as they saw their own 'flesh and blood' raped and physically brutalized. Yet the families agreed to the amnesty, the condition being that the perpetrators gave full disclosure.

How were they able to be so gracious? In the account it said that the families realized that Africa could not heal without this approach and action on their part. They had put their adversity within a greater global context and found the inner resource to forgive!

The paragraph in that chapter, which helped this lesson go from my head to heart, was as follows:-

'In the process of dehumanising another, in inflicting untold harm and suffering, the perpetrator was inexorably being dehumanised as

well' p35

In other words, if I chose to seek revenge on my father or if I chose to kill him before he could kill again, I would become like him in that moment. I would end up effectively dehumanizing him. In order to do so, I would have to dehumanize myself first, through the decision and act of killing him. This was not in keeping with my values, and I needed to be true to myself.

It was a sobering and humbling perspective, but one that enabled me to shift from a rigid perspective towards forgiveness. While I did not accept or condone the act, I decided to forgive because of who I was, because I could and because I chose to, not because of who my father was, or had become.

Forgiveness for me was all about letting go of the need to exact any revenge or hold harmful thoughts towards my father. This particular break through was a huge relief, because I understood that the only person the bitterness had been affecting was me, and not my father.

Meanwhile my coaching practice was growing. Then, as I was gearing up with the business I suffered huge financial loss. I delivered a business contract worth twenty thousand pounds. I did not get paid and I was not the only one either. The company in question had defaulted on payments and key personnel just seemed to disappear.

It was a shock to my system as well as my wallet, because I did not think people behaved like that in business. I was naïve, and at that time the loss was not sustainable, particularly as I started out with very little capital. At the same time I was paying off debt dating back to my father's trial.

In December 2002, I returned to nursing on a full time basis, in an attempt to stem the loss. At the same time I continued to build my coaching practice on a part time basis. I was head hunted for a nursing post in specialist perinatal psychiatry by a former boss from my first nursing post.

I agreed a two year period, with a view to returning to full time self-employment thereafter. However, it was to extend into a seven year run. The combination of patient care and supervisory workload, coupled with building my coaching business, took an extra toll on my energy and thyroid function, making it difficult to build momentum.

New Horizons

'You can never cross the ocean until
you lose sight of the shore'

Christopher Columbus

During that seven year period I started to see new horizons through a series of events. First of all I achieved a long term dream to work in football, particularly with Tony Adams, the former Arsenal footballer. I coached him briefly during his management at Wycombe Wanderers. I explain how this came about in the third part of this book.

This was a major achievement given that it was not easy for a female to get into that environment at the time. This happened in 2004. For the first time I caught a glimpse of my true potential, as applied to entrepreneurialism and overall life purpose.

Shortly after, when I went on retreat to Devon, I started to get a couple of strong intuitive nudges. The first one was an inner prompt that I should watch 'The Matrix'…mmm…that felt strange. I didn't think they would have any DVD movies at the retreat but when I wondered into the communal barn there were some DVDs on the shelf, and guess what? 'The Matrix' was there!

The bit in the movie that spoke to me was from the scene where Morpheus trains Neo in jujitsu. As they engage in combat Neo appears to be holding back in the fight and at one point Morpheus stops him and says:-

'don't try and hit me, just hit me....you are faster than that, don't think you are, know you are'.

I recall from that scene, making the subtle distinction between thinking and knowing. Knowing breeds certainty, and thinking breeds doubt in the above context. Decisiveness and knowingness also go hand in hand. I decided to let go of worry and applied this principle of knowing to my business goals at that point, and just knew that a business contract was imminent.

The following week I was to receive a phone call out of the blue, from a new prospect, to discuss a coaching contract. That contract was worth five thousand pounds, yet the process by which this happened was as exciting as the outcome itself.

However, I found that sustaining this certainty and 'knowingness', would wax and wane, particularly when my confidence took a knock, so it was difficult to resume my business on a full time basis. Consistent knowing proved evasive.

The second intuitive nudge I received on the retreat, was to watch the film, 'Field Of Dreams', and again the DVD was in the barn, surprise surprise! What fascinated me about this film and what spoke to my heart, was the prominent way in which intuition played a major part in the unfolding of Ray Kinsella's dream.

I knew from this that my dreams would start to crystallize, and the key to this was the requirement to open up my intuition once again. This scared me due to past associations of intuition with warnings.

In tandem with this I had taken a book with me to read on my retreat, which I felt drawn to. It was called The Millionaire Course by Marc Allen. I was drawn to this book in connection with my humanitarian dream, and it fascinated me to read how Marc was able to work his spirituality and business in harmony to make lots of money and help others.

I had been indoctrinated through church teaching about the love of money being the root of all evil, and I was sure that this was playing out as a limiting belief where my humanitarian dream was concerned.

The interesting thing about the humanitarian vision was that because it felt so big I often questioned if my mind was running away from me into a fantasy land. This is because, beyond nursing and giving to humanitarian causes on a small scale, I could not see how I could ever make that sort of thing happen on a bigger scale. Therefore I struggled to really own it. However, a bit like the nudge to write my own book, it would not leave me.

One day I was at a friend's house and decided to run it by her. I found myself in a bit of a daydream, doodling and drawing the word out in a circle, to form the middle of a mind map. As I opened my mouth to talk to my friend about the humanitarian dream my own question got answered before I could speak!

I noticed something from my doodling that was there all the time. I just had not seen it. Within the word hum**anita**rian was the name Anita!! Talk about evidence right in front of my eyes! I felt goose bumps all over my skin as I relayed to my friend what just happened, and from that day I owned the dream.

The other aspect of the book by Marc Allen that fascinated me, was how he worked smarter rather than harder, to achieve his dreams. This was a concept that I knew would be vital, yet one I found hard to grasp, as my culture and conditioning had instilled a purely hard work ethic in me. With my thyroid leaking energy this was probably something I could do with learning.

As I read this book I also received a strong intuitive nudge that I should write a book based round my journey. Shortly after, I was to be invited to contribute a chapter towards the Amazon bestseller 'Wake up Live the Life You Love'.

The other interesting thing to happen that year was to see Arsenal win the premiership title without losing a single game in the season, something that had not been done before.

Not only did I see some of the most breathtaking football to be played out by my favorite team, but I witnessed what a team of harmonized and talented team players could achieve together.

This struck a chord with me because it reminded me of my desire to work collaboratively with like-minded people, to deliver extraordinary value in life and business. Whilst I could work well on my own, it was purely an issue of fulfillment that reignited this desire.

I had somehow allowed myself to think that by contributing something of my life lessons to the amazon bestseller, I had responded to the earlier intuitive prompt about writing a book, but the urge to write my own book remained strong after this. I was not emotionally ready though mainly because I was still concerned about the effect on privacy for my family should I write this book. I was aware this would be a challenging piece of writing as it would not be academic and would involve a depth of sharing that would overrule personal privacy.

2004 should have been the year I resumed business on a full time basis, given the inspirational lessons on the retreat. However, I continued with nursing due to lack of confidence and fear that I would be cheated in business as before. In fact I stayed till late summer of 2009, and it was to take another life event to give me the push I needed.

Until that point many were hailing me as one of life's survivors. Sure enough, as I reflected on my journey from 1993 to the present, I could see the progress. I was no longer wishing to die, I had fundamentally broken free from depression, I had made breakthrough on the issue of forgiveness, and I seemed to be free of self-hate where my sexuality and identity was concerned, even though I did not know what I believed where God was concerned.

My core essence where serving and helping others was concerned had remained remarkably intact, as did my sense of humor. I was taking better care of myself and enjoying my love of playing football. I was starting to 'push the boat out', so to speak, in terms of my gifts and talents in business, and I was starting to see new horizons.

All these things should have been cause for celebration, and while I was grateful and able to acknowledge my progress, the main emotion was relief rather than celebration. That emotion was then taken over by overwhelm and fatigue. I had come so far, yet I was feeling battle weary.

Yes, my courage and determination had brought me this far. Yet I felt that it had taken every ounce of my energy to travel this far, and battle fatigue had resulted in a corrosive effect on any feeling of joy in the journey.

I had started to pull away from the shore that had kept me safe, yet captive. However I could not quite allow myself to lose sight of the shore. I needed new qualities to come to the fore for this next stage of my journey.

What bugged me was that while I had survived well, and had a minimum baseline for functioning that was high, being a survivor was not enough. I did not wish to live a life of mere existence.

I wanted to feel alive again, with an infectious energy and enthusiasm for life. My dreams needed to crystallize and re-ignite in a big way. I needed more physical energy too. I wanted to feel a sense of adventure and joy on a day to day basis, something I experienced as a young child in my formative years. I needed to find my joy in the journey of life again.

In 2009, three things converged to preface the next stage of my journey. The cumulative effect of working in a nursing environment which now prioritized politics and finance, rather than quality nursing, was destroying me at soul level and accelerating me towards burnout. Secondly I suffered a betrayal of trust in a relationship that left me disillusioned with relationships.

Thirdly, a couple of weeks later, a close friend of mine was stabbed by youths only yards from her house, just two days after I had paid her a social visit. She died from her wounds within three weeks.

It was one thing that these things happened in close succession, but the manner of my friend's death traumatized me badly, and bought back other painful memories about the murder in my own family.

I lost a lot of sleep and weight during this episode of grief, and subsequently took sick leave in order to recover. During this time it dawned on me that there is never a good time to go for your dreams. I could no longer assume that I had years on this earth given what had just happened to my friend.

I should have learnt that lesson when my brother died, yet these lessons seemed like a bar of wet soap – it was hard to maintain a decent grasp!

'The only way to rediscover faith is to exercise it'

A Narayan

It dawned on me just how much I had lost faith in people and life. This probably stemmed from when I left church, and even though I had no desire to return there, I needed to rediscover some sense of faith if I was to follow my dreams fully.

I concluded that the only way to rediscover faith is to exercise it, and so I planned my permanent departure from nursing by giving the required notice to leave. I also burned my bridges with nursing by terminating my nursing registration so I could not change my mind.

With the little capital I had, I also signed a new contract with my heart. I was going to find that place called living and commit fully to my dreams. I also decided that I was going to be bigger than any challenge that came en route, in the same way that flowing water shapes a rock over time and dissolves its hard structure.

In Hindi one suggested meaning of the name Narayan is 'moving water', and the name Anita translates at root to 'the grace of God' or 'grace'. I was going to need these qualities in abundance to help me know my name and translate it into a new reality.

I was going to learn to become like 'moving water', flowing and dissolving challenges in its path. In short I was going to live up to the good in my name, and become an inspirational force.

There was no release clause in the contract I made with my heart so there would be no turning back, and yet the whole idea of this next stage of the journey was to truly release and set myself free, to find that place beyond survival called living!

PART 3

BREAKING FREE

'So often times it happens that we live our lives in chains
and we never even know we have the key'

'Already Gone', the Eagles

THE MEDITATION

I FIND MYSELF WATCHING A BEAUTIFUL EVENING SUNSET SOMEWHERE IN Africa. As I watch the orange glow of the sunset, I feel a sense of calm, peace and centeredness. I stand here in my blue shorts and turquoise t-shirt as it is still warm. I remember that I love the warmth of the sun on my back, so I turn my back to the sun and my back starts to soak up the warm rays.

The sun begins to radiate its warmth beyond skin deep, yet without burning, and somewhere deep within me frozen blocks of ice start to thaw out. Those blocks of ice represent frozen assets, different aspects of my potential, as yet untapped, and the true extent of which I am only partly aware.

As the sun continues to thaw out those areas gently, as if it knows sudden change might shock me, so grows a new realization of my potential.

As I look on the horizon I see a deer silhouetted against the orange sky, standing still, resolute and waiting, as if in expectation. As I watch that deer it reminds me of a quote by James Allen:-

'As a being of power, intelligence and love, you hold the key to every situation, and contain within yourself that transforming and regenerative agency, by which you may make yourself what you will.'

I start to feel a new and fresh hunger rising within me as a result of this new awareness. As I continue to stand with my back towards the sun, it feels like ripple waves are emerging from me like a radiating yellow light, as if I have just connected to a powerful source and plugged into a new energy which I am now emitting.

Another deer draws up alongside the first deer and both watch me intently, as if expecting something to happen. I wonder what they are staring at. A part of me detaches from myself, so to speak, and goes to where they are standing, to see what they are seeing as they look at me.

As I do so I see ripple waves of light radiating out from me. They can actually see what I am feeling!

I now begin to see that my power to be transformed and to change my circumstances and environment are heightened. And so the setting of the sun heralds the end of a chapter and the beginning of a powerful new one.

The sunset becomes a symbol for me of the dawning of new frontiers, as I transcend my current limitations and go on to experience life at a new level.

Now it is time for me, Anita, warrior of the light, to rise and take possession of my full potential, to journey to the land called 'living' and impart that life to others, that they too may come alive.

The Gift In Constraint

I left nursing for good at the end of summer 2009. To those observing this situation logically it was a big mistake. I had so little capital, and there was no certainty as to whether I could get my business to a sustainable point before cash flow dried up. I could lose everything I had maintained from the security of a job.

However I knew that something major was missing. I needed to strip back all the distractions that were giving me the appearance of having so much without much substance. I needed to go back to the drawing board so to speak. Somehow in my departure from nursing my faith got activated and I knew things would turn out fine, no matter what happened en route.

I remembered something my personal nurse tutor once said to me. He said that we rarely ever find ourselves completely free from constraint, and that excelling in such circumstances is as noteworthy as the achievements made without restriction.

At the time those words had fed me, as I was attempting to complete my nursing qualification against the background of a murder investigation. I remember writing my last nursing essay on management and leadership. I wanted this to be my best yet.

I wrote it against the background of protracted interviews with the police. I stayed up till three o'clock every night to complete it and only just managed to hand it in on time.

My essay was marked and cross marked between two of the strictest tutors in the college, so I feared the worst. I got double A's!! I have kept that essay to this day as a reminder to myself of triumph amidst adversity, and to appreciate my capacity to bring the best out of me when under extreme pressure.

However, my decision to leave a secure career signified something different. First of all this choice and apparent constraint was my decision. Was I merely walking back into a different type of prison that was unnecessary? Many tried to persuade me to stay on in the security of a nursing career.

My response was that I needed to leave and become my own boss in order to pursue my dreams and feel fulfilled. I would rather fail in my attempt than to be left with the regret of not pursuing my heart's desire. Some understood and others seemed nervous about the response.

I could not be caught up trying to persuade others about my decision, no matter how it looked. For me something much bigger was at stake. More importantly, I was exhausted and burned out. Now I needed to be alone in solitude without distraction, in order to discover how to reignite the flame of life that had gone out.

'Constraint can develop our inner senses'

A Narayan

As I embraced the restriction of my situation and sat still with myself, I noticed and observed that my other senses became heightened, where previously they had seemed relatively mute. I was reminded of something I learned from nature.

You may be familiar with the phrase, 'as blind as a bat', when a person uses it to describe poor sight. So how does a bat 'see' where it is going, and how does it avoid bumping into objects when it cannot see?

Bats are able to hear high pitched sounds that humans and many animals cannot hear. They use their hearing to pick up these sound frequencies, to compensate for their lack of sight, and to direct them.

Firstly they produce high pitched sounds through their nose or mouth. They then listen for the echo to come back from the sound wave they produce. From the sound of the echo and its location, the bat is able to deduce the shape of its surroundings and locate any prey in the area with ease.

The echo can pick up the most subtle of movement such as the flapping wings of a fly. The capacity to pick up these sounds is also important to the bat's survival, as insects are a main food source.

It is not just the sounds, but the manner in which they echo back, which helps the bat to work out shape, size and density of an object. So this is how a bat is able to 'see' through another sense. Its hearing develops a new level of heightened awareness, and compensates for its eyes.

Somehow the confinement of my new circumstances caused me to focus on the inside and allow my inner resources to come to the fore, as I sat in stillness. I knew that stillness was crucial to obtaining a heightened awareness of my inner voice.

As I observed and switched my focus within, I started to get a clear sense of inner muscles that had wasted or gone latent. As I continued in stillness, something dawned on me afresh, and my blind spot became crystal clear for the first time.

I had disconnected with parts of my inner self in order to survive, and as a result, had blocked the full flow of life within me.

The Lesson from the Eye of the Storm

It was really quite ironic that as I determined to shed what did not serve my life, and attempted to move forward in true authentic fashion, the unresolved fears and anxieties which resided at a more subconscious level surfaced in the form of challenging circumstances.

I realized how circumstances and tangible things had come and gone in my life. I had been stripped of many things both as a child and beyond. For example I had lost friends or loved ones through death.

Even nursing was not the same in that it had now bowed to the political and financial agenda of the times, changing beyond recognition. It had taken a life event such as a protracted murder trial, to put me in a place of financial debt for the first time in my life. This was an extra layer of loss I now had to contend with.

'There is a difference between enhancing joy and happiness
through circumstance and creating joy and happiness
through circumstance'

A Narayan

Like so many people, I had allowed myself to be dictated to and controlled by circumstance, because I had invested my self-esteem heavily into external things I wanted to have or achieve. This included family, career and the ownership of certain material things.

In psychiatry I had studied the concept of locus of control, and understood the difference between external and internal locus of control where my life was concerned – in other words, what controlled the quality of my life was down to outer or inner factors. My locus of control had been weighted towards external things and my self-esteem was significantly measured by those things.

When the things I wanted to experience and achieve did not happen, this caused a downward spiral, and rather like the collapsing eye of the storm, chaotic emotions such as stress, anxiety and fear would run rampant until I found my grip again.

That grip never lasted because it was based on things that gave the appearance of stability, but not the reality of it. So my self-esteem went up and down accordingly, and I gave away my personal power to circumstance. I could never experience joy in the journey of life with that kind of gravitation.

I am not suggesting there is anything wrong with material things or achievements. However, there is a difference between enhancing joy and happiness through circumstance, and creating joy and happiness through circumstance. I needed a stronger internal reference for increased stability and consistency of experience.

It dawned on me, that whilst I fed my circumstance with worry and anxiety, I was effectively inflating them with more power, just like blowing air into a balloon will inflate a balloon. I was also inflaming circumstance by injecting fear into my perception of the situation.

The anxiety of an event or challenge came from me and not the circumstance itself - circumstances do not have emotions, they are just what they are. At the same time, I was effectively disempowering myself by allowing the situation to become bigger in my own eyes, as a result of my fear. Consequently the radius of my personal power became smaller, just like the eye of the storm.

This fresh perspective enabled me to decide to acknowledge my reality without dwelling on it. I also decided to observe current reality with curiosity rather than fear. I had to draw on my imagination, and see it from a competitive footballer's point of view to start with, in order to create a shift.

I approached it like a game of football. Sometimes a player can give the ball away to the opposing team, and then needs to win the ball back. I imagined I had given my personal power away to circumstance, and had to regain it quickly. This analogy helped me enormously. Drawing on the footballer within helped me to create a quick shift.

When I decided to acknowledge my situation without inflating it with worry, it was like letting air out of a balloon. Fear got disarmed. Honest acknowledgement of the situation was the start of regaining emotional equilibrium and personal power.

I was developing my inner 'eye of the storm'. As I continued to practice observing with curiosity, a sense of centeredness returned, and fear was replaced with resolve and a fresh sense of 'I can and I will'.

2004 REBORN

The lessons and intuitive nudges of 2004 started to come flooding back, and I knew that I needed to allow them to take root this time. I knew that I needed to close the gap between repeated exposure and frequent engagement if I was to become a skillful navigator in life.

I sensed that I needed to repair my inner foundations. I needed to exercise belief and faith to the point of knowingness, especially where my humanitarian dream was concerned. I needed to open up my intuition again and use the right brain toward whole brain application, as opposed to being left brain dominant.

Back in 2004 I was not emotionally ready to write this book in spite of the prompt to do so. I still wrestled with the public implications of writing a book, given how privacy was stripped from my family during the murder investigation.

It all came back to me now, with a stronger force than before, and I felt ready to make a start, even though I was unclear about all the details. I started to download my life experiences to date. I knew the book was meant to be inspirational and educational, in that order. That was the starting point.

I did not want this to be about telling my story per se. I wanted it to be about inspiring others with reference to my story. I still felt that I wanted a confirming signal that this was the right thing to do now, because I had concerns about whether my family would approve this decision.

In silent meditation I put the question out there, that if this was an inspired nudge, someone I respected in the personal development field would offer to read the book and write the foreword, as long as they perceived real value.

I say this because I had been advised in business to the contrary, namely that I should approach a shortlist of people, and offer them money to write the foreword for my book. The idea of this business practice, void of establishing real value, was not one I could subscribe to.

I wanted to create something based on value, and see true value exchange, not superficial negotiation and unethical practice. What unfolded over the next three weeks was simply remarkable on a number of levels.

My answer came in adversity, and at the same time showed me a different facet of adversity I had yet to really embrace.

'Opportunity can appear in the form of adversity.

A Narayan

Several weeks after I left my job I happened to injure my neck, shoulder blade and left arm, after a violent bout of sneezing. I had never experienced this before and it was extremely painful. I ended up going to the accident and emergency department of the local hospital.

I discovered later that I had experienced the equivalent of a whiplash injury. I suffered a disc bulge with such intense muscle spasm, that it required medication to release and relax the muscle. I also suffered nerve compression down my left arm.

At first I just viewed this as an injury to overcome and recover from as quickly as possible, because it felt like an intrusion on my immediate need and remit to earn money. Every action I took to reduce my recovery time failed and immobility reigned for several weeks, resulting in increasing distress.

Panic set in, an unusual emotion for me to experience. I thought I had made a wrong decision for things to turn out like this so soon after leaving nursing. I watched, as money due through business became money withdrawn at the last minute, and I feared financial meltdown.

In my quest to speed up my recovery I sought out a personal trainer, who became a friend and colleague. One day as we were chatting over coffee, he mentioned that he was going to attend a five day combat training boot camp that week, and asked if I would like to go too.

There was no logical reason to accept this invitation at that late stage, due to the injury I was nursing, the physical nature of the combat training, and the five days it would take out of my diary and wallet. Still, I loved the idea of going because it was an opportunity to pick up new practical self-defense skills in a fun and physical learning environment.

As I was about to decline, I felt this strong inner sense that I should go. 'Oh God…not this intuition stuff again', I thought.

My mind decided to put up a fight, and yet I could not squash the strong sense that I should go to the boot camp. In silent acknowledgement I said 'yes' to my intuition. I also had to be honest with my friend and inform him that I could not afford the course fee.

The combination of other pending financial obligations, and an injury that had already put me out of work for three weeks, made this seemingly impossible. I thanked him for asking though.

My friend went quiet for several minutes, and we chatted in general a little more. Then he said 'Anita you are coming and I am paying for you!' Even though I could not guarantee when I would pay him back, he insisted on me coming!

My challenge at that point, was to learn to receive graciously. I accepted, more out of wanting to embrace the lessons, than a real feeling of self-worth. The intuition that I should go had been answered, and an unexpected solution provided for me. I knew there was more to come over the next five days.

I also knew that while my perception of God was very uncertain since departing from the church, something was happening on a universal scale, whether it was God, The Universe or otherwise. Something spiritual was being stirred up and mobilized.

I still could not fully shake the panic I felt. At the same time I knew

I had to stay with the process and follow my intuition. I remembered the contract I had made with my heart, and consciously reaffirmed that decision.

There were nearly fifty guys and only three women on that course. I encouraged the men to treat me like one of them when it came to the drills, so they did!! My God, I felt sore by day three after landing on my backside multiple times. Goodbye cellulite!! More importantly, I was wondering what on earth I was doing there beyond learning self-defense skills. I got my answer later that morning.

Around mid-morning, one of the instructors called Geoff Thompson, spoke about personal power and how the Shaman tribes gather power through challenges, adversity and restriction. He added that this was something to be embraced and not feared.

I remember thinking with mock sarcasm, 'good for them', and then 'where is he going with this? I knew instinctively that this message was about to reveal the reason for my being here.

Oddly enough, I had not made the connection between the Geoff Thompson I was aware of and respected from the field of personal development, and the man that stood before me, until he started to speak.

Geoff went on to share that challenges are not automatically a sign of being on the wrong path, but would often accompany big dreams and worthwhile goals, and their principal purpose was to empower and cause growth.

I now knew why I had come. The panic brought on by my injury had caused me to doubt the decision I had made to leave nursing to pursue my dream. I was in financial free fall and felt like I had no 'parachute'.

These words became like a parachute, not only breaking the fall, but holding me up in firm assurance about the step of faith I had exercised. It felt like the wall I had put round my heart and mind was tumbling down in that moment. It was replaced with a confirming signal about the path I was taking.

Those words spoke so powerfully to my situation, and their impact was heightened by the fact that they came from someone who had learned to embrace adversity and challenges in his life. I felt very emotional at that point, and went for a walk in the beautiful grounds to shed tears of relief.

'Intuition is like a door to unexpected solutions if we respond to its call'

A Narayan

Geoff's words became like an anchor for me and an encouragement to expand my personal power. So I chose to dwell and learn to expand my personal 'eye of the storm' in the midst of ongoing challenge. I was meant to be here to receive those words, amongst other things, and my intuition to attend this event was confirmed in that moment. But it did not stop there.

I am not one to fight through a crowd to seek out a speaker at the expense of others. However I did want to thank Geoff, and just quietly prayed that an opportunity would present itself. Oddly enough, our paths naturally seemed to cross throughout the remainder of the course, and I had a brief chat with him to thank him.

During that chat I mentioned that I was writing a book. I expressed concern about how my family would view this. Geoff kindly offered to read the draft of the book when I had finished, and before our conversation had ended, he added that I should never be afraid to ask for help.

I was bowled over by the offer of help, as I could not recall the last time someone had offered me help in business like this. It had felt like an isolated path. However, his words about asking for help also stayed with me.

I remembered how I had found it hard to accept the invitation to attend this course from my friend who bought me here. I also knew that when the same message comes twice in a short space of time, I needed to grasp it. I informed Geoff that I would gladly accept his help and send him my draft.

I am not sure what I expected when I sent off my first draft. I was so used to people in business not returning calls for ages, if at all. Geoff was a famous author, film writer and BAFTA award winner. Some of his screenwriting successes include Clubbed, Bouncer, Romans 12:20, The Pyramid Texts, and Brown Paper Bag, which won a BAFTA award. His autobiography Watch My Back was a Sunday Times bestseller. It seemed logical to expect not to hear back for some time.

Two weeks later I received a call from Geoff! During conversation and feedback he encouraged me not to hold back in my writing, something I knew I had been doing. However what amazed me was when he shared that he had read most of what was out there in the personal development field, yet found my book inspiring.

He then offered to write the foreword for the book, subject to seeing the final draft. Even though the book was far from the finished article, Geoff had seen enough value to be impressed and endorse it.

Yet again, I was reminded that my minimum baseline was higher than I really grasped, even during the process of testing my skills in a new environment. In that moment I also remembered that the very thing I had asked for in silent meditation three weeks ago, had come to pass to the letter!!

When I mentioned this to Geoff, he then shared something that was to be equally moving about the miracle I had just witnessed. He explained that when he facilitates events, such as the one I had attended, he always prays that God will show him who he should help - I was one of them!!

Serendipity had showed up, disguised in adversity. I was also learning here that intuition is like a door to unexpected solutions if we respond to its call. This strange set of circumstances with my injury had led me to an unlikely scenario, which provided the answer to my prayers about my vision, without my engineering anything!!

Lessons from Adversity

For days I sat in awe of what had come to pass, and I reflected further on what had happened in those last few weeks. This event had removed doubt and took me to a place of knowing I was on the right path, particularly with regards the book.

Knowingness was a place that existed beyond belief. I was starting to feel what Morpheus had taught Neo in that scene in The Matrix. I had also witnessed the power of intuitive guidance and empowering questions, in the evidence that played out.

I had seen that intuition was not always to do with warnings, but opportunities and dream guidance too. What a relief!! I had also witnessed the effortless way in which intuition had carved out a path to answer my prayer. To someone who was a recovering workaholic, this felt strange but welcome!

'Adversity is a part of life, not an intrusion on life'

A Narayan

As I reflected further, I realized that I had missed the point of this adversity by assuming that my injury was a sign that I had made a mistake. The panic over finance, bought on by this injury, had caused me to lose perspective. That was a punishing thing to process, to believe that adversity could only imply failure and to feel that in the critical moments of my life I could not make the right decisions.

I recalled again how football had taught me that challenges can happen, fair and unfair. Even though I had learnt that life is like a physical contact sport which included adversity and challenges, I needed to grasp this at heart level.

I had dealt with my injury by drawing on the qualities of strength, determination and perseverance, to overcome it. Yet ironically, life was allowing me to go through this so I would learn that circumstance actually holds no power over me, and that I could create context from this rather than allowing context to be created for me by default.

Previously I had viewed adversity solely as a teacher, where challenges were learning situations which provided opportunity to develop character and strength.

Yet in this scenario adversity had been like a friend in disguise, confirming my path by the most bizarre circumstances. It had also been like a mirror, reflecting where I was in my relationship with myself. I had so much to learn!

By my very response, I knew deep down that the key to changing my life lay in rebuilding from the inside out, and not the other way where I was merely striving to change circumstance.

I reflected on how most things I saw through my physical eyes started off as an idea within a person. The manifestation of those things in reality was down to the creative thinking and application that bought those ideas into reality. I was now going to learn about purposeful creation, rather than creation by default.

I knew that the adversities in my life did not need to be the defining context of my life. The context I created through and from it would be the bigger picture in which all these scenarios would embed. I was starting to mobilize my creative power by shifting my perspective.

When I returned from the martial arts boot camp, my circumstances did not improve immediately. In fact they got worse. Over the next few months I was to lose my car, and just about everything, except the roof over my head.

The biggest loss was when a number of prospective clients would default at the last moment on their commitment to follow through with a coaching contract. It was very hard to replace those clients at such short notice. The corrosive effect on my cash flow meant I had less capital with which to expand the business, and therefore stabilize income. It did not feel dignifying to lean on government support to assist my self-employment.

This time I was not fazed. That in itself confirmed that I was breaking the chains of circumstance that once attached to my self-esteem. Although things seemed to have crumbled on the outside, by acknowledging my reality rather than dwelling on it, I became more aware of the solid inner infrastructure that was forming. Rather like the changing of the guards I was learning to master situations rather than be a slave to them.

Change can often seem chaotic. I could not make out what was happening in this chaos, yet the image of a tapestry reminded me that the knotty threads that form the back of a tapestry, reveal a clear picture on the other side.

That was accompanied by a strong sense that these circumstances were only temporary, and would turn round. As if to confirm my thoughts, I found myself picking up a Buddhist magazine from a shelf one day. As I flicked through its contents, my eyes fell immediately on a sentence that said:

'Though right now you may have appeared to have suffered
a loss, if you persevere in faith, you'll be able to recoup that
loss tenfold'

Those words became like another anchor for me during this life transition. Soon after, I experienced another serendipitous event.

This came about as a result of an instinctive nudge to buy the book 'The Eureka Enigma' by Ron Holland. I was aware of who Ron was, but had no direct contact with him. After I read the book, I felt compelled to get in touch with Ron, to offer feedback and thanks for the lessons I had picked up from the book as it related to my journey at present.

Again, I was not expecting an immediate reply to my email, but I received a quick reply with an invitation to meet up. We traded notes, explored and shared overlapping themes from our journey.

What was interesting for me was that Ron, like Geoff, spoke a lot about intuition as a driving force in his journey. He also spoke about the value of stillness and visualization, and how consistency of practice is the key to the unfolding of dreams.

Ron also offered to read my completed draft and gave me valuable feedback with written endorsement! This felt like deja vue! Key people were coming into my environment, and intuition was a recurring theme.

By the third completed draft of my book Geoff could see the progress and transformation. For me though, something still felt missing. What was it?

In the film Gladiator, Maximus finds himself going overnight from a high ranking trusted general in the king's army to a slave, where he is forced to entertain the new emperor in the Colosseum. Fighting to the death was the name of the game in this arena.

This new emperor had dethroned his own father and ordered the murder of Maximus and his family. When the new emperor discovers that Maximus is still alive, he arranges for him to die in the ring by unfair means, but Maximus somehow survives.

In between fights he is kept a prisoner in chains. When the emperor's sister privately visits his cell, to engage Maximus to fight against the tyrannical reign of her brother, Maximus tells her 'I could be murdered tonight in my cell or killed in the ring tomorrow. What difference can I make?'

'The essential message of constraint is that circumstance holds no power to keep a person down unless they allow it to'

A Narayan

Maximus could only see the constraint of his imprisonment. What he failed to notice, was that every time he was in the arena he won over the crowd. Even in his confinement he was exerting power to influence the crowd. That power to influence came from within, and not just from the battles he won in the arena.

Somehow I knew from the constraint of my situation, that there was something about myself I needed to grasp, and that the person I needed to win over was me. This would be essential to completing the journey of coming alive again, with a security and momentum, from which the book would write itself with greater depth.

As I continued to reflect and ponder on what it was I needed to see from my new place of awareness, I had a growing sense of revelation. The essential message of constraint is that circumstance holds no power to keep a person down unless they allow it to.

The earlier storm was no longer simply about uncovering a murder and overcoming trauma. The storm was like a vehicle with a new picture emerging. The resounding message was of a new and exciting future.

Repairing The Foundations

I knew that deeper insights lay in the dream I had, foretelling the murder, and so I returned there and reviewed its contents with my new sense of awareness. I now saw the parallel nature of its message with clarity.

As you recall, the dream had foretold a highly devastating event with a promise that I would not be destroyed even though I might feel otherwise for a while. The second theme of the dream is where I wish to focus because it revealed the inner profile of a child who had to become an adult far too quickly. In doing so, childhood became suppressed, as part of a survival strategy.

What came with that, was a brave person who had a strong sense of self in so many ways but not a deeply loving relationship with herself, as a result of the emotional poverty she had experienced.

My parents had taught me about morals, respect and dutiful responsibility, which was valuable. However, the expression of love and care was heavily weighted toward duty and obligation, which typified my cultural background.

It was heavily punctuated with dos and don'ts. Love was expressed in transactional fashion rather than unconditional fashion, with little warmth or emotional depth.

'You can only build as high as your foundations grow deep'

A Narayan

The strong sense of myself had enabled me to survive. The formation of a deeply loving relationship would be paramount to finding that place called living because I needed to experience the belonging and intimacy of an unconditional love from myself first of all.

It was a subtle, yet powerful difference. I needed to close the gap between strength and love.

The part of the dream that had the most profound effect on me was the bit where I noticed the small child which was a younger version of me. As I revisited that part of the dream I started to cry as a huge awakening came over me.

All I wanted to do was to protect and love that child. If I would not emotionally abuse that child, why had I done that to myself thereafter? After all, that child was a part of me still, even though I was now an adult. I was not to blame for the abuses I suffered in childhood mainly from my father, but I was responsible for what I was and did to myself thereafter.

With great remorse, it dawned on me that my quiet self-loathing was like a form of self-abuse, even though it was a conditioned response. I had absorbed past experiences into my self-esteem and unwittingly taken the baton of abuse, and run with it. In doing so, I was effectively colluding with the same behavior I had fallen victim to and had denounced during my family experience. The only exception was that I was not physically violent toward myself. This behavior and response was perpetuating the vicious cycle of self-abuse.

It was a shocking and sobering insight. My initial interpretation and reflection on the dream had revealed self-neglect. Self-abuse went deeper and I had never perceived self-hate as a form of self-abuse until now. There was a thin line between self-neglect and self-abuse and I had crossed it. It was a profound and powerful insight, yet crucial to my freedom.

In that moment I knew I needed to forgive myself and shed that behavior, as I did not truly own it. The moment I asked forgiveness from my 'inner child' was the start of creating a nexus based on true self-reconciliation.

I needed to learn how to give myself the gift of a deeply loving relationship, operate from that place, and create life with a powerful new purpose. This deeply loving relationship was the hub state of a strong inner eye of the storm, and also a center piece for purposeful creation.

I had learned in life that you can only build as high as your foundations grow deep. Just like a tree, I needed to learn how to put my roots down deep into unconditional love so that I could draw life in abundance, with creative and powerful self-expression. How was I going to give myself something I had not received or learned properly?

I knew that love needed to replace fear. Love and passion are a powerful creative force. They hold the seeds for fulfillment in life. On the other hand, fear and passion are toxic in their combination, and can kill growth in its tracks. I was gaining a heightened awareness of the gap I needed to close even if I did not yet know how this translated in detail.

I started to scan my foundations afresh. I reviewed the mental process I had used and refined for personal growth from my nursing days, which had taken me from self-reflection to an outcome I wished to achieve – see diagram below.

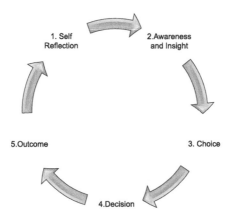

In terms of what I did well, I understood how reflection led to self-awareness and insight. I could see how new insights led to new choices, from which different or new decisions could be made to affect a particular outcome.

In psychiatry, I remembered the teaching about self-disclosure and feedback, laid out in the The Johari Model. It was a two dimensional model designed to increase self-awareness, and I had practiced it well. I had a great working knowledge of how mental defense mechanisms worked such as projection, displacement and rationalization.

I was known for my high empathy towards patients, which enabled them to open up quickly and experience therapeutic benefit. I understood that in communication, the main message received is through body language and tonality, rather than the words that are spoken, something I cultivated to great effect with my patients.

This is because I saw them as human beings who were unwell, rather than patients with conditions. My reputation for being humane and empathetic, along with skillful application of mental health nursing, spread in ways I was unaware of.

In terms of what I needed to improve on I knew I had to get to know myself afresh, and the question I asked of myself was, 'How could someone who knew her mind, who displayed such mental strength and agility, show such emotional poverty when it came to the relationship with herself?'

When I reflected on my career in psychiatry, I recalled being taught the importance of a non-judgmental attitude, as well as maintaining positive regard towards our patients. However, the emphasis was on the mental aspects of health, with scant attention towards the other layers that impacted health. I guess that is why they call it mental health nursing.

'Our relationship with self is like a lens through which we view and shape the world'

A Narayan

I noticed that I engaged with my mind in a 'matter of fact' manner and never allowed myself to feel the corresponding emotions. My experience and reflection of myself was through the mirror of my strongest mental traits - perseverance, courage, determination, resolve, and a disciplinarian mindset.

These strengths were the traits of an overcomer, and the persona it related to was a warrior. Although these were strong assets, I used this 'lens' through which I viewed myself to an extreme extent. In expanding these qualities alone, other aspects of viewing and experiencing me diminished, moved to the edge of my inner awareness, or disappeared from sight.

This overplay of strengths prevented me from seeing other aspects of me that were out of balance. I needed to address these blind spots.

The insight from this observation suddenly became apparent. I had shut off to the emotional and spiritual side of myself significantly in order to survive, because I was afraid of those things. Fear was filtering out important insights.

It was the manner of my reflection rather than the technical process of reflection that was erroneous. It was such a subtle distinction, yet one I knew would make a huge difference. The following analogy from the golf course, demonstrates this powerfully.

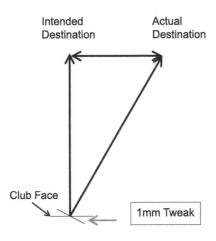

I remember when I first started to learn golf at the driving range. I was taught how to align the club face, in order to hit the ball to a point straight ahead. If the club hit the ball as much as 1mm off center, the overall distance between where the ball landed and its intended destination would be significant.

The subtle distinction and insight about the manner of my reflection, was like a 1mm tweak that I knew would make a huge difference to the direction and reach of my life from here.

With fresh perspective I saw that the relationship with self is like a lens through which we view and shape the world. I was looking at myself and the world around me through a fragmented sense of self, which was limiting my growth and achievement.

The double edge sword for me was that even in this limited scope, I was growing and achieving beyond those around me. My so called strength had also become my blind spot.

I had associated my own emotions with weakness and vulnerability, and had traded these for strength. I associated spirituality with church, and had traded this for self-sufficiency. My strength and self-sufficiency had ultimately contributed to burnout, as I had relied heavily on a few inner resources. The altruistic nature of nursing had only added to my experience of burnout.

Now I was going to learn that vulnerability and interdependence were strengths, as scary as that seemed right now.

On a fundamental level, I knew that I needed to adjust my self-perception. As I shifted focus to my inner resources and wondered how I could develop a deeply unconditional loving relationship with myself, my sense of strength for the journey ahead increased. Like a detective who had found a fresh trail of clues, I had an extra skip in my step now.

I knew I needed a new perspective of self that I could own. As I meditated and reflected on how this could happen, a picture and symbol emerged that reminded me of the meditation at the beginning of this part of the book. I saw an image of radial waves coming out of me like a ripple effect with four distinct phases as below:-

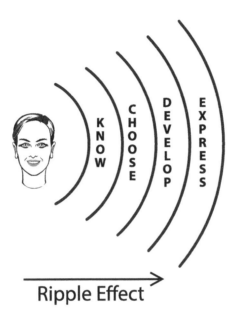

Ripple Effect

Immediately, the picture seemed to click and take on meaning for me, in similar vein to the dream I described earlier in the book.

As I looked at the picture in reverse, I could see how each stage connected, and how difficult it would be to achieve and express my dreams authentically, when my self-knowledge was so one-dimensional and devoid of love.

It would be very difficult to embrace my gifts and talents from that place, let alone develop and create something that would make for meaningful self-expression in this world.

The picture very much described a process of alignment and congruence, where each part affected the next part accordingly, and where the energy at each point either became diffused or strongly consolidated, depending on my alignment.

I discovered that the manner of my reflection needed to be more holistic in order to develop greater accuracy of thought. It became clear to me that accurate reflection was more than just a mental process. This was both a process and a skill, which would draw on my imagination as well as my resolve.

This is how I adapted the manner and process of reflection, as a result of the self-discoveries made.

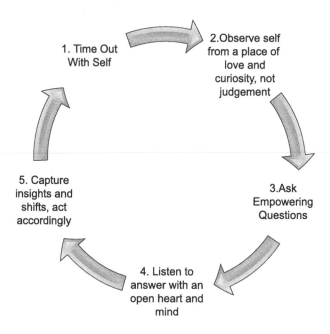

In summary it was about:-

1.   Being

2.   Observing

3.   Asking

4.   Receiving

5.   Responding

This is how each aspect weaved itself into each of the four stages detailed next, and more importantly how I started to thrive and blossom as a person.

Ripple Wave 1 - Know

It was the Greek philosopher Socrates who coined the phrase 'know yourself' and another Greek philosopher Aristotle who stated that 'knowing yourself is the beginning of all wisdom'.

From the reflective cycle above, I knew I was good at spending time alone. I needed to build on that by accessing a stillness that went beyond silence, for greater regeneration and awareness. I focused on deeper relaxation through meditation to bridge this gap. Growth and change takes place best from a composed state, so this came to be what I called a first base principle.

It was the second part of the cycle that presented the biggest challenge though. I knew that I needed to shed the warrior mentality with its duty bound expression of self-love, and find another perspective that would help me know myself at a deeper level.

So I went back to the dream and observed it with curiosity rather than judgement. I wondered about the 'little warrior' that had become battle fatigued, burned out, and bereft of life. Was that burnout simply circumstantial? Circumstance had played a significant part, but I noticed more, as I gazed on.

The True Nature Of My Burnout

Many who observed my journey from a distance would say it was understandable that I burned out, due to the weight of circumstances I carried over a period of time. Their definition of burnout mimics the commonly held view, of a physical depletion of energy that results in dysfunction.

In other words, my ability to regenerate from the onslaught of challenges that came in quick succession was severely impeded, leaving me with a residual energy deficit.

Although this definition has valid mileage, I knew in my case that the roots of burnout went deeper, and that I had to understand the things within me that had contributed to this state. What I came to observe from my state was that burnout starts at its roots with disconnection from self, whilst thriving is about an integrated expression of self.

DISCONNECTION WITH SELF

When I look back, I could see how past events had conditioned me to perceive myself through a disciplinarian, austere, and obligatory type 'lens'. I grew up with a father who did not work for the most part of our upbringing, but gambled, along with a mother who was a workaholic.

There was no balance between the two extreme role models, and I gravitated towards being a workaholic because it seemed more morally acceptable. My career was where I invested my emotions and my identity, just like my mother appeared to do.

I found it difficult to play and enjoy myself without feeling guilty, because I had never learned that work and play could exist in harmony. I always saw them as conflicting and incompatible states. That was the perception I developed through observing my parents.

I could see how the infectious joy and love I had for life as a small kid, slowly leaked and defaulted to a mode of existence that was based on meeting my parents' expectations. Culture and expectations from significant others had acted as a powerful suppressant.

This eventually led to disappointment, confusion, lack of direction and fulfillment, abandonment and disconnection later on, when choices about work, relationships and lifestyle kicked in.

The disconnection happened slowly and in a very systematic way. My rules eventually became based round seeking the approval of others in order to fit and meet my need for belonging. By default, I did not really have ownership of my life. As a result, I lost sight of being a person in my own right.

Any glimpse of my uniqueness was suppressed under a layer of fear, as I swung between self- expression and seeking approval from significant others.

Self-sufficiency masked vulnerability. Career and achievements started to define me more, as I tried to compensate for the inadequacies and craving for self-worth and acknowledgement. Instead of filling the gap, these external things had a corrosive effect. Instead of resolution I got the illusion of happiness.

My mental strengths became a smokescreen for the underlying corrosion of self-esteem. Whilst there was nothing wrong with the mental characteristics and high standards I displayed, I cancelled it out via my relentless perfectionism.

When it came to the relationship with me, I was highly critical and judgmental. I lacked empathy and very rarely celebrated progress, because in my mind I was here to deliver results. This hypercriticism and self-flagellation acted as filters, denying other insights and experiences to express themselves. This blunted self- growth and creative expression. My mental traits were inadvertently causing me to fall apart.

Defragmentation Of Inner Resources

I overplayed my mental strengths whilst suppressing love, joy and peace, amongst other emotional assets. Faith also got suppressed amongst other spiritual resources. I was a master suppresser of emotions, because I equated emotional expression, especially painful emotions, with loss of control. Like the warrior I was always equipped and ready for battle, even when there was no battle to fight.

The murder only added to my hyper vigilance and agitation, although I hid it quite well. Underneath, anxiety was etching away at my inner lining, causing extreme discomfort.

'The body always reflects what lies beneath'

A Narayan

It is interesting how spiritual commentaries refer to underlying spiritual themes of trust and perceived threat, when exploring the different autoimmune illnesses I experienced, such as Thyroid Disorder, Myalgic Encephalitis., Psoriasis and Urticaria. It seemed to be corroborated in my experience.

In an autoimmune illness the body continues to remain in fight mode long after the threat has passed by. The analogy of the warrior was not lost on me. The body will always reflect what lies beneath. My body felt like it was registering unexpressed emotion and perceived threat.

Suppression had denied me other important resources for life, and the experience of myself was narrow.

Much of today's teaching in therapy and personal development does not help. One aspect of a person tends to get over-emphasized above another. Positive thinking is an example of this, where the emphasis is on thoughts. It is very difficult to think clearly with wisdom, when there is trapped emotion for example. That's a bit like expecting a pus infected wound to heal.

Things are often taught out of context. I commonly come across the phrases 'I put my heart above my head' or 'I put my head above my heart'. The question is, why should our inner resources be in conflict? At the end of the day we possess a body, mind, spirit, emotions and soul.

'The capacity to come from an integrated sense of self is key to thriving and failure to do so, causes gravitation toward burnout.'

A Narayan

I do not believe these were given to war with each other, but to work in harmony, and yet seldom do I hear the encouragement to work these inner resources together in an integrated fashion. Isn't that what wholeness is about?

The capacity to come from an integrated sense of self is the key to thriving and failure to do so, causes gravitation toward burnout.

DISABLING ENVIRONMENT

The other factor that had been instrumental in my burnout was my environment, starting with family, where the constant theme for many years was survival, as I battled to remain authentic and true to self.

The cumulative effects of conflicts in role modeling, death threats in the face of authenticity, and the rollercoaster of volatile emotions which was on constant display, meant that long after I left home, I was entangled in much of my conditioning and very confused.

In addition to this, my nursing career was a high output one, as I was constantly dealing with the emotional distress of people who were unwell and afraid of the clinical environment in which they were nursed. The underpinning principles that governed nursing when I first qualified got systematically consumed in the five organizational changes over fifteen years.

The political and financial dictates of the time threw quality nursing into disarray. Moral and ethical conflicts ensued to the point where I became soul destroyed by the changes that made nursing less recognizable over time. The demands on nurses outweighed the dwindling resources.

It became increasingly difficult to blossom as a nurse whilst maintaining self-preservation. Any attempts to uphold the true identity of nursing at grass roots eventually came at great cost, namely to my health.

POOR CAPACITY TO HARMONIZE INNER RESOURCES

The capacity to harmonize inner resources is an issue of integration, relationship and balance, and one for many years that I lacked, due to over-emphasis on certain traits to the neglect of others. It was very difficult for me to orchestrate all my inner resources when I lacked capacity to entertain certain aspects of my being.

Also, I was aware from observing my father, that everyone has a scope of behavior – how they behave when they are at their best, and how they behave when at their worst. There are many factors that affect that scope such as stress, communication style and resourcefulness.

My capacity to narrow that scope toward my personal best became eroded over time as a result of a disabling environment and diminishing self-esteem.

Personal Best ← ———————————————————— → Worst
Scope of Behaviour

It very rarely showed in public. Only the discerning and astute may have noticed any disparity. Many were too self-absorbed to notice, which suited me fine at the time. The level at which I felt apart from my personal best, was more about how I felt within myself emotionally on a day to day basis.

At my best, I was engaged, humorous, fun loving, and energized to make the most of life and inspire others. At my worst, I would be withdrawn, fatigued, demotivated, impatient with myself, inflexible, and quietly resentful when others did not show themselves to be remotely dependable and consistent in behavior.

Poor Capacity to Receive

I think it is fair to say that the demands of my personal and professional life meant that I gave out a lot. One of the aspects of burnout is the inability to recover sufficiently in between output and input. Recovery is not just a question of physical relaxation, depending on the output.

In my case it was also about the capacity to dissolve and let go of conflicting emotions, brought on by the situations I found myself in on a personal and professional level. It was about my capacity to process things in a way that contributed to increasing resourcefulness. It was about regaining perspective where conflicts were common at work.

One of the difficulties I encountered was that when adverse circumstances played out so thick and fast, I was often left on catch up for quite some time. The speed at which I needed to regenerate was too fast. In addition, I did not have the inner resources to keep up with the pace of challenge, and often found it hard to receive because of my trust issues.

The words and encouragement from Geoff about asking for help kept playing on my mind. I knew that had I not responded to the kindness of a friend to attend that martial arts event, and had I not responded to Geoff in sending him the draft of my book, I would not be sharing this with you now.

I knew I needed to build on the concept of receiving, yet was acutely aware that I had to go beyond technical application, and engage with the art of the process. Giving and receiving are part of the same cycle. Giving cannot happen without receiving, and vice versa. My starting point had to be to give and receive from myself in areas where I had denied myself love and care.

Building Bridges

Understanding the nature of my burnout was one thing. The act of building a bridge toward recovery would be another thing which would not establish itself overnight.

I return now to the cycle and manner of reflection. I pondered as to 'who' should replace the little warrior that had previously been my persona. As I reflected and engaged my imagination, a new image and persona presented itself to me…enter the best friend.

'The biggest divorce I have witnessed is not the one that
takes place between two people, but the one that happens
when a person disconnects and splits from themselves, as
a result of damaged self-esteem. We need to reconcile with

ourselves and become our best friend'

A Narayan

This was the angle from which I would now view myself with curiosity and love. I chose the best friend analogy because somehow, a parent or partner did not seem appropriate given my history. In fact there are more dysfunctional families with high divorce rates than not.

However, behind those statistics is a more silent theme playing out. I call it the silent divorce. The biggest divorce I have witnessed is not the one that takes place between two people, but the one that happens when a person disconnects and splits from themselves, as a result of damaged self-esteem. We need to reconcile with ourselves and become our best friend. This seems to be a more harmonious analogy to use in general.

When I thought about it, the place where I spent the most time was not in the workplace or asleep. The place where I spent the most time was in my own skin. I take that person with me wherever I go, so if I am not comfortable in my own skin, I transmit that subconsciously in any situation.

I knew that the way I communicated with myself needed to be accompanied and aligned with a tonality and a body language that supported love and an energy that could only come from genuine love.

As I imagined how a best friend would behave toward me, I was able to gain some insight as to how to reconcile with myself.

When I thought of my close friends, I knew that what made them special were shared values and the opportunity to spend time alone with them. In a special friendship I could chat about anything and be myself. We could also be silent together and just enjoy each other's' presence, which gave significant depth to the experience.

This was my starting point. I decided to spend time alone in silence, to listen, experience and observe myself with curiosity, not judgement. I needed to engage my imagination a lot at first, in order to really step into the world of a best friend and observe myself from that place.

At first the shift in perspective bought tears to my eyes, as I saw with fresh insight how toxic my emotional state had been, and how hard and cold I had been towards myself as a consequence. Growing up quickly had equipped me for the adult world, but I never got to experience childhood with much freedom.

As I was able to make the distinction, namely that I had responded to a conditioned image of myself, rather than the true person I was, my compassion turned to curiosity.

As I stayed with this process over a period of time, I started to notice what my close friends had observed. Only this time I was eager to embrace it. Instead of just feeling safe in my own company and the silence, I began to feel and enjoy real companionship.

It was quite a profound shift in observation and it was enabling me to feel a genuine appreciation for myself. This got me thinking about a branch of science relating to physics. Quantum Physics explores the effect of energy on matter at a sub atomic level. This scientific view point holds that all matter emits energy which can be measured as a sound frequency [hertz], including human thought and emotion.

It is often referred to as the subtle energy field because it is not perceptible to the human eye or ear alone, yet observable and felt in terms of effect on perception, reality and behavior. Quantum Physics had opened up a world of experimentation regarding how observation affects matter, suggesting that the way one looks at something impacts both perception and reality.

The field of Cymatics seeks to explore the fascinating theme that the object of that observation can also be impacted by energy. Cymatics is the name given to the visible study of sound and vibration on structure. Experiments visually focus on how energy as a sound frequency can alter the structure of matter. For example, there are many you tube videos demonstrating the changing structure of water when exposed to different audio tones.

As a football player I understood how the experience of passing the ball can feel different depending on how composed or anxious I felt. It also affected where the ball landed.

I had not translated this to the relationship with myself until now. It felt like the loving way in which I was now observing self was affecting and igniting my cells with life. I was developing a deeper appreciation of the significance of different thoughts and emotions on personal experience from a subtle energy perspective.

This new perspective of being my best friend became like a tuning fork. Self-observation was accompanied with feeling. Self-attunement developed on a physical, mental, emotional and spiritual dimension. A new peace started to arise within me along with a sense of joy and happiness.

These things were there all along. I simply had not accessed them because I had been looking in the wrong place. It was like a blind spot. I was so conditioned to believe that circumstance and significant others were the prime providers of these states.

It reminded me of drilling for oil. Once technology identifies an area of potential oil, it is not visible at surface level. Therefore it is necessary to drill several layers beneath the earth's surface before the oil can be accessed.

Likewise, the many protective layers of conditioning around my heart had caused the rich vein of life to become buried and invisible within me.

Emotional states such as happiness are also like precious commodities we possess, but layers of conditioning have made them hard to access immediately. I had to peel back the layers of resistance to discover what had been there all the time.

I had habitually searched for happiness as if it existed outside of me, when all along, it was there deep within. It was a commonly held belief that the world was flat until Christopher Columbus discovered it was round. The earth being round was not the new thing. It was the discovery of something that already existed that was new….and so it was for me.

Vibrant emotional qualities were there in abundance, deep within me, waiting to be discovered, but I had to stop chasing them like the greyhound chases a rabbit. I did not need the permission of circumstance or others to feel these things. I needed to allow myself access and in doing so I was now getting in touch with my own personal power.

Not all the observations I made about myself were entirely new. What was different was the ability and new found capacity to appreciate those things and who I was as a result. As I continued this process I noticed how I had defined myself through labels such as career, gender, sexuality, and culture.

These labels seemed hollow and like a piece of clothing that I had now outgrown. I was growing toward a new self-definition. I wanted to identify myself by the values and characteristics I wished to build my life on, and those by which close friends knew me. It was not hard to define those values. I just had to notice what was important to me, and what others saw in me - empathy, generosity, courage, love, joy, fun, authenticity, resilience, compassion, humane, to name a few.

I knew that circumstances could change, but no-one could take my values from me. These values were to form the spine of my self-definition from here on. This would not only give me a sense of security, but would give me a solid platform and foundation from which to grow and blossom.

The starting point of developing those values was to be those things to myself, and now I could see the connection between the relationship with myself and my dreams with greater clarity. For example, I needed to be humane towards me in order to achieve my dream as a humanitarian contributor. I also needed to give myself the gift of an inspired life, if I was to inspire others with my life. My dreams would become a natural extension of the relationship with myself.

I meditated and reflected on this further. It was the process of redefining myself through my values that was to sever the 'ball and chain' that had weighed me down where my sexuality was concerned.

While I had engaged in romantic relationships since my departure from church, they were accompanied by resignation rather than any sense of peace, love and self-acceptance. Now for the first time in my life, the focus on my values enabled me not only to stop fighting myself, but more importantly to embrace that person within the context of a new self-definition.

At first I felt sheer relief, and then relief changed into a feeling of liberation. Needless to say, when I disclosed my sexuality to my closest friends, they did not bat an eyelid or treat me differently. They just saw me as a person in my own right.

Why did I think it would be any different, that somehow they would reject me? I was seeing my friends' responses through my own doubt and fear. That is a classic example of how the relationship with myself was acting likes a lens, shaping my perception, but not necessarily with accuracy.

Now my values were providing a bridge between the old and new relationship with myself, along with both a new found stability and a real sense of freedom.

I also decided to write a letter to myself, as I would a best friend, relaying the joy of that new friendship. I posted it to my home address. I have read and kept that letter to this day.

I started to feel lightness in my spirit that I had not felt in years, and it felt good. The key to emotional consistency on a day to day basis lay within my capacity to be my best friend and access wellbeing from within.

This new way of relating to me formed the context for more accurate reflection. It was a way of being, and a powerful lens that was to dissolve overly harsh and critical thinking, so that more empowering insights could filter through.

Ripple Wave 2 - Choose

In the context of the best friend analogy, I knew that a true best friend would notice my good qualities and gifts, and would point them out to me.

Of course, a best friend would also be honest and tell me things sometimes that were not easy to hear, but the difference would be that it would be done out of love rather than to put me down. My friend would hold the image of the best of me, even when I was unable to do so.

A best friend would acknowledge my gifts and talents in a way that might elude me, because they would view me from a place of greater objectivity, and not through the filters I placed on my self-esteem.

'Choosing yourself is where you really acknowledge and
appreciate your uniqueness '

A Narayan

For me choosing yourself is where you really acknowledge and appreciate your uniqueness, your talents and gifts in a meaningful way, knowing you have a significant and unique contribution to make to the world should you decide to act accordingly.

So few take the time to really appreciate who they are and what they bring to life through their own personal journey. I could see how lack of appreciation had been tantamount to taking myself for granted, resulting in self-neglect up till now.

I was starting to see how getting to know myself as a best friend informed the basis of true self-acknowledgement, and that to choose myself is to acknowledge, appreciate, embrace and endorse my uniqueness. It goes beyond mere self-validation.

I needed to acknowledge and embrace my uniqueness, along with my gifts and talents, in a way that continued to nurture and fan into flame the life that had now started to appear.

I decided to create a mirror to aid more accurate self-reflection and monitor my progress and growth. On this subject I created a simple yet powerful exercise for myself. I took a full length mirror, and with complete eye contact, started to observe, appreciate and express how much I loved myself, along with as many things I observed about my qualities, gifts and talents.

The reason to use a full length mirror was to observe my body language in full, as I spoke. As a minimum I used a bathroom mirror so I could watch facial expression, particularly eye contact.

I knew that when I could talk to myself consistently, with confidence and authenticity, without flinching or losing eye contact, as I would to a close friend, I would have mastered this area sufficiently. It was not easy at first. I used my reflective cycle in tandem with this process, and practiced both silent observation and companionship, along with dialogue.

With practice over the following months, I watched myself disentangle, open up and talk to myself in a way whereby tonality, body language and words became more aligned. It felt more than just good when I finally got there. It felt liberating.

This is an exercise I give to my coaching clients too, and you can do it too. It is very powerful because a mirror gives you more immediate and dynamic feedback through direct observation in real time. For me it is more powerful than a questionnaire. It is a great tracking tool at the same time.

In terms of acknowledging my gifts and talents, the clues were in my life. For example, I could see how my fascination with the mind, my love of helping others and my passion for football, could translate into coaching specialties in accelerated learning, peak performance and health.

I could see how my skills in verbal and written articulation could result in representational work in industrial relations cases, speaking, and writing a book. The list goes on. Now I was acknowledging them with a heartfelt appreciation, as well as understanding afresh that what made their expression unique was me!

RIPPLE WAVE 3 -DEVELOP

I saw the process of developing myself as twofold - becoming and creating. It is not a new concept. The Italian renaissance humanist, Pico Della Mirandola, talked in depth about the importance of creating when referring to the development of man.

I came to understand how I could start to blossom in my growth when my roots were embedded in a loving knowledge and appreciation of myself and my gifts. I realized that it was not possible to develop those things properly without developing a proper self-partnership, as I was the key factor in applying this.

The gifts I identified more easily were empathy, listening, compassion, humor, verbal and written articulation, teaching and advocacy. Others would need uncovering through further reflection.

In the past I had developed my talents, yet left myself behind in so many ways. I went about my achievements in rather mechanical fashion. The difference now was that my development would be infused with a love and joy that had been missing before. My energy would be more harmonious than scattered. I would be able to enjoy the journey of growth.

In terms of gifts and talents, I knew with fresh clarity that I could not ask the world to see or acknowledge what I was not prepared to see and acknowledge in myself. I knew that the process of creating self was a process of becoming, and would be more than just a set of tasks that required completion.

The process of developing a sound infrastructure that would hold the outer reality I was attempting to create would be an ongoing one. It would be a dual process of self-development and skills development, in order to apply knowledge effectively.

I took inventory of my emotions and looked to see how I could expand my experience of love, fun, joy and peace, for example. The idea in expanding these was also to navigate other emotions such as frustration and disappointment, with greater ease, fresh perspective and proper context.

As far as gifts and talents were concerned, I looked at the things I was good at. I looked at what I loved. I looked at the environment in which I wanted to exercise them, and considered what gave me joy and fulfillment too.

Where these four lines of inquiry converged and overlapped, these were the areas I sought to focus on. The four areas of skill I started to identify and develop further were coaching, teaching, writing and speaking.

I sensed the need to find a new and fresh expression for my skills beyond the typical service type approach, but I was unsure as to how I could do that.

'You can't gain momentum on limited inner resources any more than you can drive a car at high speed in second gear'

A Narayan

I also needed to replace the patterns within me that had contributed to burnout in the past, and learn to work smarter rather than harder. More importantly I wanted to experience fun and create momentum at the same time. That would require a whole brain, whole heart approach rather than relying on a left brain approach, which I had previously been accustomed to.

I knew from owning and driving a car that a six gear car is not meant to be driven in two gears only! Yet I had only used a fraction of my capacity and potential. I knew therefore, that you can't gain momentum on limited inner resources any more than you can drive a car at high speed in second gear.

HEALTH

In keeping with the car analogy, I wanted to develop mirrors for my health for better functioning. It seems odd that we will put our cars through an MOT and service on a yearly basis, because it is a legal requirement, even though it makes practical sense given the wear and tear that comes with increased mileage and usage.

However, we do not do this for our bodies and overall health. For me my health is a more important vehicle than a car, and while the National Health Service does not cater for proactive checks, I decided I would do so myself.

I decided to 'clear the decks' from a health and symptomatic point of view. I also planned to build mirrors to measure the progress of any solution I applied on a physical level. This would help me increase the energy baseline from which I would address the more fundamental root issues.

The technologies I decided to use for starters, as mirrors and measuring tools for any process I applied in 'before' and 'after' fashion were:-

- Live Blood Analysis – profiles state of the cells
- Cardio Pulse Wave Technology – profiles the state of the heart [non-invasive]

The value of live blood analysis for me is that although it is not a diagnostic tool, it acts like a mirror, giving a picture and profile of the state of my cells. I wanted to promote my health at cell level so I decided to use live blood analysis as a 'before' and 'after' tool to measure the effectiveness of any solution I applied. I was able to see the effect on the cells of drinking more water for example. The change in cell profile was clearer, round and free floating as opposed to sticky and less round.

I considered cardio pulse wave technology to be a more accurate measure of blood pressure as it measures the wave from the base of the heart out to the periphery and back. Traditional blood pressure machines only measure the pressure of blood in the arm. I understood the significance of blood pressure in heart health.

With the above technologies I could start to observe, plan and adjust toward wellness with greater accuracy.

MEDITATION

I knew that spending time alone was an important part of getting to know myself. I also needed to increase my capacity for energy and resourcefulness. This would not only help in my continued regeneration, but would also help me navigate through life with greater ease. It would help me maintain focus on my dreams too.

I had experienced something of the connection between relaxation and awareness and needed to cultivate this for increased wellbeing.

I had benefited greatly from silence on a regular basis, and found it to be highly regenerating after all the noise of traumatic circumstance. However, I knew I needed to go further. There was a difference between silence and stillness, the latter contributing significantly to insights and creative solutions.

For me, whilst silence represented the absence of noise and external distraction, stillness was about dissolving the mind chatter. It went beyond mere physical relaxation. Meditators often refer to it as the emptiness, a place of letting go of thoughts, a highly creative place. So I worked on developing those four aspects as in the diagram below.

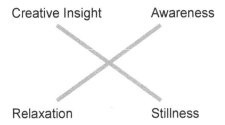

Creative Insight · Awareness · Relaxation · Stillness

It is interesting that in business, the logical technique of brainstorming is underlined and emphasized, yet I rarely see the practice of silence and stillness as valid processes for creative solutions.

Maybe it has something to do with the lack of tangibility that surrounds this activity. People are more comfortable with the ritual of being seen to do something, even if it does not equate to productivity and effectiveness.

I was not interested in how my process looked to the outer world, or whether I fitted in with the status quo any more. I was interested in what created greater value and effectiveness.

I remember when I first started meditation, how I felt energized afterwards. Now I was taking a more eclectic approach to meditation because I was still not finding it easy to concentrate for long periods, since the murder, as I was accustomed to in the past.

It seemed that concentration was the last piece of me to come back in recovery terms, and it was both slow and sporadic. So I interspersed manual meditation techniques with brain wave entrainment technology.

Brain wave entrainment is a form of sound technology that trains the brain to produce more alpha, theta, delta and gamma brain waves, by introducing sound frequencies that match those brain waves. The idea is to listen passively through headphones. Focus and concentration are not essential requirements, unlike other forms of meditation.

I found brain wave entrainment to be very powerful alongside my other practices. This formed the bedrock of other skills development, because I understood that if information and new learning is to take root, it is easier when you are in a relaxed, aware state, which equates to the alpha brain wave state. This is the basis of practices such as hypnosis and hypnotherapy.

'Stillness goes beyond mere physical relaxation, allowing the inner eye to expand in observation and insight'

A Narayan

I noticed that when I relaxed to the point of stillness, the greater my awareness, vision, creativity and resourcefulness. A great analogy for explaining the power of relaxation is the 'magic eye'.

If you have ever done the magic eye exercise, you know that when you look at that 'magic eye' picture, and relax your eyes to the point of being in a daydream, you see the picture in 3D. Stillness goes beyond mere physical relaxation, allowing the inner eye to expand in observation and insight.

From a place of relaxation, I also wanted to expand my awareness, as opposed to shifting focus, in order to reduce stress and reduce my scope of behavior for greater consistency.

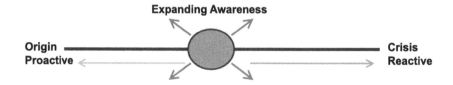

If I could expand self- awareness towards the point of origin, where stress was concerned, I would be better placed to nip it in the bud. This proactive approach would also counter the more reactive approach, where stress is only dealt with when symptoms became more obvious and indicative of a mounting crisis.

I wanted to learn to anticipate crisis better, and prevent accumulation of stress. I also knew that the more relaxed I became the more I would create an environment for more awakenings and insights to occur.

EMOTIONAL RELEASE TECHNIQUES

I decided to add a couple of processes to my armory, that would enable me to identify and release trapped emotions, residual and present. I liken trapped emotion to pus in a wound. It infects thinking if not released.

One of the most powerful processes I have engaged in is kinesiology, following the recommendation of a close friend. Kinesiology uses muscle testing as a mechanism to feel the subtle energy field within and identify subconscious messages that may be playing out in self-communication, especially beliefs.

For example, in past sessions, I found that when I held my arm out horizontally and verbalized a statement that was true for me, my arm remained firm under slight applied pressure from the practitioner. When I verbalized a statement that was not true for me, my arm would go weak under slight applied pressure.

This informed me that while I could consciously override certain limiting beliefs and emotions, others were more deeply engrained and needed uprooting. It was valuable to have a process that tested out alignment between my conscious and subconscious beliefs. It meant that I could work with more accurate information.

In tandem with kinesiology I started to use 'clearing' techniques. There are all sorts of clearing techniques out there. One of the most common processes is Emotional Freedom Techniques, which utilizes tapping of the finger on meridian points to help clear stuck energy associated with trapped emotions.

Whilst I have tried many processes and techniques, the one I have come to use more often is a spiritual practice called ho'oponopono. As I understand it, this is a process of releasing toxic energy and deleting erroneous messages from memories. My attraction to this process came as a result of reading a book called 'Zero Limits' by Joe Vitale and Doctor I Hew Len.

I was intrigued and inspired to read the account of this practicing psychologist who used the process in Hawaii to assist in his therapeutic work with the criminally insane. That hospital is now closed as a result of the healings that took place, which is accredited by many to Doctor Len's work.

As someone who used to work in psychiatry, I was fascinated and naturally curious to test this process out. I wrestled with some aspects of the concepts laid out in the book, but I decided to run the process as an experiment, as with all other processes outlined.

What I have observed so far is how certain unresolved emotions have neutralized or dissolved, and that my intuition appears to have sharpened. Instances of 'knowingness' are becoming more frequent, as a result of clarity coming through. The experiment continues.

Whole Brain Thinking

On a practical level I acquired the skill of accelerated learning to help me take in new information. Studies I had come across showed how it outperformed traditional learning by a factor of two to one, making learning easier.

I first came across accelerated learning when I embarked on my coaching qualification in 2000. I wondered why this had not been taught in schools, such was the relative ease of learning I experienced.

Accelerated learning is a whole brain process, whereby anyone can learn anything fast. In traditional education students are taught topics. On the other hand, accelerated learning teaches the student how to learn in a way that aligns with how the brain learns. That learning can be applied to any topic.

The key components covered by the process are mental preparation, absorption of information, comprehension of information, recall of information, testing knowledge and reflective learning.

Whereas traditional learning only engages certain parts of the brain, accelerated learning teaches you how to deploy the brain's different intelligence centers in an integrated manner. This allows a person to learn with ease, develop competency, confidence and speed.

Abraham Lincoln is commonly quoted as saying "Give me six hours to chop down a tree and I will spend the first four sharpening the axe."

He was referring to smart work as opposed to hard work which is normally measured by volume of time and effort. Smart work refers to the processes which leverage time and effort, such as mental preparation and effective tools. Accelerated learning is one of those processes that act like a sharp axe to learning. You get through more learning in less time, with greater precision.

It made my learning so much easier, and enabled me to pass my coaching exams with limited time during my recovery, with a pass of 86%. This has become one of my coaching specialties, from which many have benefited. My nephew passed his police exams with 96% after I taught him this. A client I had nursed from severe post-natal illness went on to pass her 'A' levels a year later. It was and is a powerful smart tool that I have kept and developed in my skills closet.

The other aspect of whole brain application that I had to reconcile was the area of intuition. I knew that intuition connected to the right brain, and that this had been an area of shutdown for many years, due to past painful associations of intuition with warnings and adverse events in the main.

'Intuitive guidance can cut through years of effort based on left brain application alone'

A Narayan

However, I was slowly starting to see that those intuitions were also protective in nature. Since leaving nursing, I started to notice the other facets of intuition. I have already shared how I came to meet Geoff Thompson, via an inner prompt which set off a chain of events up till the time we met. As mentioned earlier that was not the only one.

I knew and had enough evidence that intuition would play a crucial role in the unfolding of my dreams. I understood how intuitive guidance could cut through years of effort based on left brain application alone.

However I needed to make peace with myself and the universe at large concerning this gift. I found that this resistance naturally dissolved as a result of the process of self-reconciliation.

Now that I had revived my self-esteem, I could appreciate the gift of intuition I had been given because of the responsibility and integrity required to exercise it in difficult circumstances. It was in fact a compliment to my standing and growth at that time. This new formed association enabled me to shed the label of 'punishment' that I associated with intuition in the past.

One of my favorite accounts concerning intuition is from the bible is in Luke chapter 5, where some of the disciples and fisherman had been fishing all night. As hard as they tried, they were unable to catch any fish. In the morning they were frustrated, tired, and ready to quit.

Then Jesus suggested that they throw their nets into deep water to catch fish. As fisherman they thought they knew their expertise best, and considered the idea futile and illogical. However, they gave in and applied the suggestion. Their nets nearly burst from the amount of fish they caught!

This account always reminds me of the power of intuition, and the extraordinary things that can happen as a result. I cover a couple more magical events that transpired as I developed my intuition, later on.

In the meantime, what was interesting to note from previous examples cited, was the way in which intuition and serendipity worked hand in hand, and the effortlessness by which certain doors opened, where years of sheer effort alone had failed.

If I return to the example where I met Geoff Thompson, there was nothing logical or rational about the path that connected us. If I had used logic to meet him, I probably would have looked him up via his website and arranged to attend one of his events, which would involve training and travel costs.

Under normal circumstances I would not have chosen to go on such a physically intensive event off the back of the injury I sustained to my back and neck. As far as financial priorities went it was both out of reach and a luxury item in my opinion. The situation seemed impossible and the decision unwise.

What fascinated me about the intuitive message to go was how it flew in the face of conventional wisdom to create a bridge and open the door to serendipitous outcome. It was as if a wider field of intelligence got triggered and went to work outside of my conscious radar.

The nature of intuition is such that there is no evidence to support it. It is a felt thing accompanied by a strong certainty. I was discovering that intuition behaves like a gentleman, inviting me to follow its message. The inner eye of intuition sees beyond the human eye, and does not lend itself to rational inquiry. Its voice is subtle yet strong, and requires partnership to open doors. My part in that is to surrender to instinct, to trust and follow my inner guidance, in the absence of logic. This lays down the tracks for circumstances to be orchestrated in an effortless and seamless way toward a purposeful outcome.

If there is a key message I consistently take from watching intuition at work, it is how it provides a seamless gateway to infinite possibilities and resourcefulness that are off my conscious radar, as I learn to work in harmony with it from my heart.

The Energy Differential

The effortlessness of intuition intrigued me, and I started to review my own personal effectiveness, which had historically been more weighted toward effort, hard work ethic and left brain thinking alone.

One physical learning experience that helped me further experiment with energy and effortlessness, was when I was taught how to break through a plank of wood with my hand, at a personal development talk during a sales conference. Martial artists commonly perform this feat with wood or a stack of bricks.

I recall offering myself as a volunteer because I loved being physically involved in learning. I was taught briefly how to break the plank of wood, and for the first ten attempts I got it wrong. I was nearer to breaking my hand than breaking the wood!

'Effortlessness is connected with the subtle use of energy'

A Narayan

The instructor stopped me and helped me to understand that I was trying to break the wood from the strength of my arm, rather than come from the energy center of the solar plexus. The Chinese refer to it as the dantian.

Apparently, I needed to visualize my hand as already through the wood. In tandem I needed to hold that image as I followed through with my hand, drawing from the energy in my solar plexus region. Two more attempts later, I was successful. What amazed me more than the result was the fact that when my hand went through, it felt like breaking through polystyrene rather than wood.

My hand did not hurt! How could wood effectively feel like polystyrene? The 'place' I had come from energy wise, had given me a different experience with the feel of the wood, than from the strength of my arm alone! I had been taught how to 'sharpen the axe' of my energy in this scenario!! This was another example of subtle energy at work, as explored in the field of Quantum Physics.

This experience stayed with me, even though I had to return to it to absorb the lessons at a deeper level. Simply translated, I was learning that the place from which I took action was as important as the action itself.

I also understood that I was working with my energy at a deeper and more subtle level in this scenario. Since then, every time I have practiced from this place I have found that effortlessness is connected with the subtle use of energy.

The enlightenment was that every time I took action from a place where self-love, belief, knowingness and joy were present, the whole experience of taking action and accomplishing results felt easier and quicker.

I was starting to tap into a source of energy within myself and learned to direct it to achieve things I never thought I could do, and the experience felt different for doing so. What else could I create and do of value from this 'space'?

Empowering Questions

This is probably the single most powerful technique I have used in my life, and I was starting to use it in my 30s, well before I understood its power. For me an empowering question is a positive one that adds to the quality of my life and creates value.

The use of this technique was responsible for the opening of an opportunity to work with Tony Adams, the former Arsenal and England football player, in 2004. It was a huge dream, and I simply asked the question verbally and in writing as to how I could do some work with him.

By an overlapping set of circumstances that played out we got to meet, and I got to do some coaching work, after which I received a glowing testimonial. That is not to say that it was given to me easily.

I was supposed to have an interview with Tony to explore how my skills could assist him as a manager along with his team. When I arrived for the appointment another official of the club interviewed me instead.

I was asked many questions to determine my knowledge and application of football.

Fortunately I had prepared and reflected well, which was not a stretch for me in one sense, but I did need to be clear about the value and benefit of my services, so my preparation was more to do with articulation than content.

The man that interviewed me apologized afterwards, and said that it was necessary for me to go through this process as they were accustomed to seeing low quality people and propositions. However, in my case I had clearly impressed them and this led to a meeting and subsequent coaching work with Tony Adams.

I share this detail because the success of the interview was not merely down to asking an empowering question. The question opened the door. Here is what I learned about questions.

The act of asking a question is not too dissimilar to putting a keyword search term into a google browser. The search bar will return a whole host of related searches to the keyword entered. When I ask a question, particularly when I ask a question out loud, my brain will seek to answer that question and bring related possible answers into my field of awareness.

The great thing about empowering questions is that you can use them at any time, in any place, irrespective of your status and growth. I have found it to be a simple yet profound technique for directing focus towards creative solutions, and increasing the quality of my life in general. Empowering questions can enable that one millimeter tweak in thinking that creates shifts and significant results over time, as described in the golf analogy earlier.

Some of the most powerful questions I engage with involve asking for awakening and inspiration. This is because the answer and insight I receive bypass the conscious mind and deposit a certainty, an insight, and a life force where growth and achievement are concerned. I have found it to be a powerful precursor to decisions.

OPENNESS OF HEART AND MIND

I discovered three essential ingredients to receiving answers - emotional readiness, being present, and an openness of heart and mind. Emotional readiness usually indicates and prefaces change and solutions to questions. The act of being present is essential to noticing answers, and openness of heart and mind are an important part of receiving and embracing possible solutions.

I found the more I asked different types of questions of the same situation, the more the questions would be like mirrors, creating different angles for reflection. The process of asking different questions also helped me to break the rigidity of my thinking and foster an open heart and mind.

This rigid mentality was one of the 'prison bars' I described earlier. I was simply reconnecting with the 'Christopher Columbus' approach I experienced as a child. This would allow me now to see outcomes as mirrors, where I could tweak, adjust and change my direction depending on what transpired, and got reflected back.

A successful outcome would depend on my response in terms of wisdom, discernment, decision and actions. I was learning from my journey that decisions were more powerful than intentions, as long as I could let go of the need to get everything right, and cultivate an explorer's mentality.

Repeated Engagement

On the subject of learning, I had read a lot and listened to a lot of personal development. However I had not been as good at repeatedly exposing myself to the key lessons. More importantly I believed that if I was to become a skillful navigator of life I needed to grasp that repeated engagement is even more powerful than repeated exposure.

The only thing that counted was not what I knew, but what I applied to great effect. All other knowledge was effectively redundant.

'repeated engagement is even more powerful than repeated exposure'

A Narayan

As I re-engaged with the inspirational accounts I had read and revisited lessons that had helped me, I was to gain a fresh appreciation of the power of repeated exposure and frequent engagement, where reconditioning was concerned.

Bruce Lee recognized this power when he said 'I fear not the man who has practiced 10,000 kicks once, but I fear the man who has practiced one kick ten thousand times'

That phrase would have inspired the warrior in me many years ago. However, I wanted to apply it within the new context and persona of being my best friend. I have found that the more I practice proactively in private, the more easily I am able to access those skill sets when needed in different situations.

Building From Strength

I returned to other aspects of my life where I had learnt this in order to work from a place of strength, and transfer the lessons across to other aspects of my life. Football had been a great teaching ground for me.

I had learned in football to do the basic things well through frequent drills, and this lesson had followed me in life. However I needed to improve further, so I revisited some of the lessons. The following are some of the key lessons I started to transfer with greater application.

What Football Taught me About The Game Of Life

I often get asked how football can be compared to life given that it is a game, whereas life is not. Life is very much a game by virtue of the fact that we set rules for personal living, whether deliberately or by default. Those rules are closely associated with our beliefs. They determine the scope of our lives, and how big the 'playing field' of life becomes.

Therefore they also determine what is possible for us to experience in our lives, and by the same token also indicate what can't happen. When we allow something to happen in our lives, we also disallow other things.

So we need to be aware of the rules we set for living, and how they mark the boundaries of the playing field of success. If they are preventing us from living life successfully, it is important to become aware of them. Then we can re-examine and put ourselves in a position of choice, to change the rules and change the outcome, or accept the constraint.

ARE YOU PLAYING TO WIN OR ARE YOU PLAYING NOT TO LOSE?

This was the biggest learning lesson on the football pitch, and one which when I grasped, changed my life profoundly. This lesson is best described from two very different competitive football matches I played in.

I recall my first public competitive game at 26 years old when I played for Bury St Edmunds. We were drawn to play against Dunstable in the FA Cup. Dunstable were clear favorites to win and were also strong contenders to progress far in the competition. As this was my very first competitive match since leaving home, I was itching to make up for lost time.

Football Debut For Suffolk Bluebirds at 26yrs

After joining, I broke into the first team very quickly and played as a center forward. At that point I was relatively unknown to my team as well as the opposition. This was a typical cup game where the underdogs were playing the giants.

The game was played in the grounds of the upper school I attended on a sunny autumn day, and twenty of my church friends turned out to watch. All in all, it made for quite an idyllic and emotional experience.

I had 'fire in my belly' and a huge desire to wreak havoc on the opposition, by playing to the potential that had got me into the first team. I decided to play with belief, fearlessness and sheer abandonment. I was not going to worry about mistakes, but play to my strengths and express my skills.

I played the game of my life and got known very quickly after that match. The cup giants were humbled as we beat Dunstable 4-2. I scored a hat-trick, in what became a memorable first debut and performance, and one that saw me fast tracked to play for the region.

I was 'in the zone' and everything I did on the pitch that day seemed to go right. I was mobbed at the end by my team mates in pure celebration. I had played to win, and we had won.

The only thing that stopped me becoming the leading scorer for our team that year was a debilitating virus I played on through. I only just missed out on becoming the top scorer for the club. I had been given another angle from which to view my high minimum baseline of performance. It was a great first season for me.

Now compare this to the first competitive game I played for Basingstoke. I had not played for a few years while I completed my nurse training, due to shift work. As before, I broke into the first team very quickly and played my first match at thirty years old.

I was with a new set of players, and for some reason my mind became preoccupied with not losing my place in the team. I did not want to fail on my first appearance for Basingstoke. Subsequently I was tense and made the most glaring errors during the match.

For example the timing of my tackles would be off, resulting in more fouls. Simple short passes would not reach my team members due to the tension causing my muscles to contract. Some of my decision making was checked by hesitation, resulting in missed opportunities to penetrate the opposition incisively. I ended up playing one of the worst games ever, with minimal expression of my true potential. My performance was poor by my own standards and I was upset afterwards.

During my reflection of the game, I identified that I had held back for the sake of playing safe in order to win a regular team place. I had played to avoid losing, rather than playing to win. The resulting anxiety and contraction in my energy caused my muscles to tense, and I started to play 'within myself' and deny myself full expression. This killed my performance.

Two different games saw two different mindsets and emotional states, and therefore two different outcomes.

History should have taught me to prepare as per my first game. Maybe the loss as a result of the murder and recent trial had carried a subtle under current into my performance this time round.

Fortunately, I had the capacity to reflect with accuracy on my game and get to the root of the problem. The answer was not to train harder, but to make a decision from that day on to play big and play to win. This also involved separating my self-esteem from the latest traumatic circumstance.

From that day my game transformed. As the result of the decision and shift I made, I won many 'player of the match' awards along with regional selection.

My playing career extended well into my forties with great success, as captain and player for club and region. I became renowned for my dependable and consistent performances, and was considered part of the spine of the team.

I picked up the manager's player of the season for three consecutive seasons, something that had not previously been achieved at the club. It all started with the decision to play to win, and express myself with authenticity.

When I left Basingstoke to play for Caversham, we narrowly missed out on promotion, finishing joint top of the league. My versatility led to playing in midfield and later in central defense.

In life, when fear overtakes desire, or security overtakes fulfillment, the mentality of playing not to lose will feature as the likely scenario.

I have often been asked about what was behind my success on the football pitch, particularly in the latter part of my career. Apart from pointing out the value of playing big, the other key to my success was my capacity to reflect accurately on my performance from game to game.

After each game I would go home and reflect on what one or two things I did well. Then I would ask myself what one or two things I could do differently, or improve on in the next game. I would reflect in that order.

This is because most of us are conditioned to talk in terms of strengths and weaknesses. We tend to notice what we do 'wrong' more easily than what we do well. This is equally a self-esteem issue, and it used to be the case for me. The purpose of this reflection was to redress the balance in order to develop a more accurate perspective of my performance.

It also enabled me to be highly focused in the next game, by playing to strengths and working on the one or two things I reflected on for improvement. This type of reflection helped me to grow as a player, as well as to develop consistent and mature performances.

———

Most players of my time never reflected in this way, and their response to any training issue was simply to train harder. Accurate reflection had given me fuller expression of my talent as well as competitive advantage. Belief in my ability also played a huge part in my success on the field.

It was to take a while before I transferred these principles effectively to other parts of my life. In business, I decided to let go of the need to dwell on and absorb intimidating behavior. Furthermore I would stand tall, believe and focus on my principles and values without apology. When I started to apply this more consistently in business, amazing things started to happen as I describe later.

The key here was about being myself rather than trying to fit in with the status quo. With this in mind I also looked at my personal life. I decided that I would not defer to a less evolved state and settle for second best in order to be in a romantic relationship. I had succumbed to a belief that maybe the relationships I had experienced up till now were as good as it would ever get. I needed to shed that belief and create a new reality. I decided from that moment to only consider a potential partner in the future if they had sufficient emotional and spiritual depth about them, that would support my personal evolution and vice versa.

I was learning to let go of the need to fit in without apology. It enabled me to feel fresh hope for a future romantic partnership that would be highly evolved and fulfilling. This made me feel better about conducting business too.

Give Yourself Permission To Make Mistakes

On the football pitch, I found that when I gave myself permission to make mistakes I made fewer mistakes. As counter intuitive as this may seem, what I was doing effectively was disarming the tension of possible mistakes, and allowing my humanity to come through.

What happened as a result of removing that pressure was that I started to relax physically, as I shifted from dwelling on not making mistakes to merely acknowledging their possibility.

From a more relaxed and composed state, I started to get the best out of myself and achieve with the consistency required for optimal performance. I was operating more from the alpha brain wave state.

I understood the difference in the dynamic between performing to my best and perfectionism. Nobody is perfect, and perfectionism carries pressure and tension that is unreal. Adrenaline then starts to flow in excess and pulls against best performance.

The perfectionist rarely accepts praise and never feels that their best is good enough. They never enjoy their progress. This is how I used to be, and something I continue to work on.

I started to use brain wave entrainment in tandem with meditation to frequent the alpha state so that I could address subconscious blockages, be at my best, and perform likewise when required. My proactive practice enabled me to develop greater resourcefulness and composure and access them more quickly in situations that demanded them.

WHEN YOU EMBRACE CHALLENGES YOU GET PAST THEM QUICKLY

On the football pitch I was fearless when it came to heading the ball, but I noticed many were uncomfortable with that part of the game, and this was not just in women's football either. I had no problem with heading the ball, and understood the danger of heading the ball incorrectly.

If you tense up and let the ball drop on your head rather than go to meet it, it hurts and you can damage your neck muscles too. However if you open your body up and go up to meet the ball with equal force it does not hurt, and you can redirect the ball with power and impact.

I scored as many goals with my head as I did with my feet, because I was comfortable heading the ball and I also retained great capacity to redirect the ball from different parts of my head.

Although I had accepted the lesson from football that life is like a physical contact sport, I was still holding my breath through the challenges, so to speak, and shrinking somewhat, as if to put up with it.

I had not met adversity head on for the most part. Instead of embracing it, I tensed up and passively navigated it. As a result it made challenges more difficult to navigate and prolonged suffering at times.

Once I started to transfer this lesson over to life, I noticed I gained in resilience and strength. This helped me to navigate through adversity with skill from a more centered place. Things did not faze me as much, and I was able to see the bigger picture of my life purpose. As my overall vision and resilience grew it started to trump any challenge.

LIFE IS NOT A REHEARSAL

Anyone that plays competitive football will tell you that training sessions take place weekly or twice weekly as a minimum. This is where fitness and skills get developed. However I knew that even though life was like a training ground in the lessons that got served, it was no rehearsal in that no single moment repeated itself.

It was unfolding in real time, and it could teach me a lot as I embraced each moment, in order to grow, create and achieve my dreams. One of the challenges I needed to overcome was that my life had either been preoccupied with unresolved issues from the past, or I was dwelling on anxiety about the future. I was unable to be in the present moment for any length of time.

My focus swung like a pendulum between the past and the future to such an extent, that I would frequently go 'absent without leave' [AWOL].

This is a term used in the army where a soldier escapes his post in dereliction of duty without authority to do so. It is also a term used in psychiatry where a patient absconds from the ward without permission. This stance was reflective of the survival mentality that had been my mode of operation for so long. The key to successful living was to engage with the present.

When I started to see my identity through the values I wished to build, and when I grasped that emotions such as peace and happiness were immediately accessible from within, I was able to enter the present more often. I also started to see how this emotionally vibrant state could build a powerful bridge to helping future dreams unfold.

Football Is A Team Game and So Is Life

One thing football highlighted quite strongly for me was how team and collaborative effort could achieve so much more than individual effort alone. I remembered reading about how a flock of geese could cover 71% more distance when flying in a 'v' type formation.

Football never took away my individual talent, but gave me fuller expression within a team as well as a feeling of fulfillment and joy that came from togetherness. When I was in survival mode the isolation of my journey led me to think that life was a very individual path where the fittest survive.

Basingstoke Town FC at 36yrs   *Caversham FC at 37yrs*

This idea was compounded during my work in psychiatry. The thrust of all therapeutic input was to help patients back from dependence towards independence. In reality, none of us live totally independent lives, even the most fiercely independent amongst us.

For example, we rely on the news and weather to give us basic information. We may turn to friends for help from time to time. In effect we live more interdependently, and maybe it is this that should be fostered. It is about learning to give and receive.

However, whether I was alone or with others, I had come to appreciate the importance of having the right people around me in my life. Just as I played against opposition better than myself in sports in order to develop my game, I have learned to surround myself with friends who reflect my values and display them to an equal or higher level, so I can keep growing.

The team perspective has also given me a greater appreciation of what connects me to others and my environment, rather than what separates me. It has also helped me to learn to integrate my inner resources as one team, rather than working them as isolated components.

In a world that emphasizes competition and individual survival,

John Donne's quote 'No man is an island entire of itself', reminds me otherwise. Harmonious working is valuable and powerful.

Andrew Carnegie, the great steel mogul of his time, accredited his huge success in business to the ability to surround himself with those who had the required expertise he lacked, along with the capacity to enable them to work cooperatively toward a common goal. It was out of this process that the term 'mastermind' came to formation and practice.

As I developed the above areas, I found that my belief, faith and knowingness increased. I was expressing myself with greater freedom and less fear over taking risks. I was making decisions without succumbing to the anxiety to get things right. This is because I started to grasp the essence of success. My success in life was guaranteed, not when I achieved something, but at the point where I embraced myself, my gifts and decided to play big with my life. Achievement would simply be confirmation of my growth and decision.

I was developing more of a partnership approach in all things starting with self-partnership. I began to see remarkable things express themselves whilst working with the above principles of alignment, along with building value and cultivating relationships.

Ripple Wave 4 – Express

'Full expression is the natural manifestation of playing big'

A Narayan

For me, expression is the natural combination of knowing, choosing and developing. It is about contributing and giving to my life and the world, through creating and delivering value. Full expression is the natural manifestation of playing big with authenticity.

On a personal level there can be no giving without receiving. On a business level, that translates into the exchange of value between provider and client.

When I decided to transfer the lesson of playing big on the football pitch to my business, I enlisted the help of a couple of mentors briefly, and extracted useful guidance with regards positioning, whilst safeguarding the need for creative expression in terms of content. I reviewed the whole coaching process as traditionally taught. I concluded that I needed to form my own template and system, to plug key gaps that my own journey had exposed, and also to reflect the expansive value of that journey.

'If it is possible for leaves and clay and wood and hair to
have their value multiplied a hundred, yea a thousand fold
by man, cannot I do the same with the clay that bears my
name? Today I will multiply my value a hundredfold'

Og Mandino

I wanted to increase and multiply my value to the world, through distillation of all the principles and processes I had applied and tested out in real life including adversity. I wanted to develop a system with a set of powerful guiding principles rather than rigid formulas.

In order to understand the coaching ethos behind the system I created, it is worth highlighting a few of the challenges I discovered with traditional coaching.

When I first completed my coaching qualification in 2000, the traditional coaching process used was based round the SMART model.

For those of you who are unfamiliar with this, SMART stands for specific, measurable, attainable, realistic, and time framed. This framework was designed to validate and measure goals and goal achievement.

> 'success is like a coin – the being and doing aspects are directly linked'
>
> *A Narayan*

One of the things I noticed in particular with my personal application of the model was the lack of enjoyment in the journey, and how this impacted the outcome. This is because the model, by its very nature, emphasizes the doing aspects of goal achievement.

It only addressed one dimension of success, and while everyone has their own definition of success, I discovered that success is like a coin – the being and doing aspects are directly linked. Accomplishment and lasting success depend on developing and integrating both sides of that coin.

Given that the place I spent the most time was in my own skin, and the only thing I truly had was this present moment, any coaching process had to be pertinent and effective where these core issues were concerned. These were issues of 'being' that needed equal emphasis in the definition of success.

When these areas are addressed, the emotional vibrancy experienced in the present directly impacts the whole process of goal achievement. By this definition, goal achievement becomes a confirmation of growth and success, not the creation of success.

THE LAW OF ATTRACTION AND PURPOSEFUL CREATION

The other problem I encountered related to the framework for goal achievement, and I want to comment on that with reference to the law of attraction which got popularized in 2006.

From my life experience, I first got introduced to the power of human potential when I walked across hot coals, at a Tony Robbins Mastery University in 2000. As you know I did the 12ft and the 40ft walk.

The SMART model really did not do justice to this feat, just on the 'realistic' or 'attainable' aspects. However this was my first experience of going deeper with my own potential whilst learning to orchestrate my inner resources to perform the feat.

In 2006 'The Secret' DVD and book got released, which saw the popularization of the law of attraction.

The message of The Secret laid out in the foreword of Rhonda Byrne's book is that 'The Secret can give you anything you want' The caveat to this is that you need to align your thoughts and emotions consistently, according to your desires, such that you magnetize and manifest your desire in reality. This is the essence of the law of attraction.

There were many collaborators to the book that appeared on the DVD testifying to the power of the law of attraction in their lives. Examples of profound healing, dream achievement and material wealth were amongst the many true stories shared.

As much as I was inspired by the various testimonials relating to manifestation and deliberate creation, I struggled with the way the law of attraction was being taught. It seemed to lack integration. The teaching appeared to portray the universe as some sort of vending machine and I could not subscribe to this image. Neither did I believe that you always get what you want.

Take the example of Abebe Bikila. Abebe was the first black African to win Olympic gold in the marathon. He did so in bare feet in 1960 and 1964. An injury forced him to stop part way through the next Olympic marathon.

However in 1969, a car accident left him paralyzed, and although he did everything he could to heal and recover the feeling in his legs, his healing was partial. His dream was cut short. Not one to live a defeated life, he took part in an archery competition for athletes who were confined to a wheelchair.

He tackled his injury with as much grace as his running, because he accepted that adversity was as much a part of life as triumph and winning. His life was cut short at forty one years old, due to a brain hemorrhage, resulting from the residual head trauma as a result of the car accident. Over seventy thousand people attended his funeral; such was the legacy of inspiration he left behind.

Bernie Ecclestone carved out his success in Formula 1, but not in the way he first imagined. His original intention was to become a champion in Formula 1 racing, having left school at the age of sixteen years.

Unfortunately a major crash bought his career as a racing driver to an end. His dream was short lived. Yet rather than write his dreams off, he went on to build the second biggest motorbike business in Britain before changing over to motor racing. He became a prominent figure in Formula 1, and his income streams were made in cars, teams and sponsorships.

Bernie Ecclestone did not get what he wanted when he wanted, but carved out his success by looking at other possibilities in his industry of equal or greater value. He was able to adjust his focus and give fresh context to his life based on a perspective of value.

Martine Wright was injured in the 7th July bombings in London, while travelling to work. Her injuries were such that both legs were amputated. In the 2012 Paralympics, she represented GB in the women's team event of sitting volleyball. GB lost in the opening round to the Ukraine. However Martine was able to embrace the opportunity and occasion with gratitude.

I doubt it was in her script to lose her legs. She managed to convert her trauma over time to an experience that enabled her to inspire others by adjusting and showing what happens when you focus on ability rather than disability.

For me, I wanted to play competitively for Arsenal Ladies Football Club when I was younger. However the ban on my playing competitive football by my parents meant that I did not really start playing for a league team until twenty six years of age, by which time I was on major catch up.

My desire to become a detective in the police force was unsuccessful too because I did not meet the minimum height for women. That rule has changed since then, by which time I had moved on into psychiatry.

In the film Field Of Dreams, Doc Graham shares with Ray Kinsella how he narrowly missed playing in the major league in baseball, and then trained to become a doctor.

Ray replies 'it would kill some men to get that close to their dream and not touch it, they'd consider it a tragedy'

Doc Graham responds differently when he says, 'Son, if I'd only gotten to be a doctor for five minutes, now that would have been a tragedy'

Does all this mean we should not go for our dreams? No, not at all. However I would suggest, we also need to learn to apply knowledge in context, navigate disappointments, and discover different avenues of expression for our dreams based on equal or greater value.

'The quality of the relationship with yourself will determine
the quality of your life'

A Narayan

Ultimately while you do not always get what you want, you do get who you are. The two can overlap but do not necessarily equate to the same thing depending on your self-image and corresponding beliefs where success is concerned.

The quality of the relationship with yourself will determine the quality of your life. It is not a luxury item where your life and success is concerned and I am not the first to conclude this. The late Maxwell Maltz, famous for his book called Psycho-cybernetics, which addresses self-image, concluded in similar vein. Ignore this at your peril.

For me, there seemed to be a lot of context and alignment missing from 'The Secret', which stripped the potency of the message in key places. However, it was an interesting and valuable springboard, from which to experiment with, and fine tune my own process.

I am not going to make a law from my conclusion about the law of attraction, and what works. I offer my process. However, by now you should have grasped the importance of running and testing things out in your own life, like an experiment.

Do not accept anything as true, even the things I have said, just because someone has said it. It is important to foster ownership and responsibility. Otherwise all you have is mere adoption of knowledge with no ownership over your life.

At the end of the day the only knowledge that counts is that which you are able to apply to great effect and progress in your life. The variable in all processes is you, and the effectiveness of any teaching and learning methods. You are unique and so is your own growth.

The law of attraction is a powerful law which I apply within a context of authentic partnership, playing big with meaning and purpose, and being expansive in the way I create and deliver value through my life and gifts.

CREATING VALUE

Having shared the problems I encountered with traditional coaching, two experiences gave context and shape to the proprietary system I devised. The two transformational experiences were walking on hot coals and breaking a plank of wood, which were described earlier.

What these two experiences taught me was that the brain learns faster than I think it does. Also when I come from an integrated place within, my experience of the process and the outcome are entirely different and more effortless.

Up until the experience with hot coals I did not believe it was possible to walk successfully across 12ft or 40ft of hot coals with only two hours instruction. I thought you had to condition yourself over a long period to an elevated state of mind to be able to perform this feat. The plank of wood experience was not merely about visualization or being multisensory. It was about working with the different dimensions of self, combined with subtle energy application. It affected the experience of the process and the outcome.

The UP System is a concept, a template and a system, designed to raise the quality of the relationship with yourself as well as the quality of your life, including lifestyle and dream achievement.

It is a true inside out system that builds round the spinal points of alignment, acceleration and accomplishment in an integrated manner. It addresses you in the now as well as you in the future through the four stage ripple effect process drawn earlier. Heart intelligence is cultivated, not just brain intelligence.

The being and doing share equal emphasis. It brings a balanced and integrated approach to success by placing equal importance on the place from which you take action, not just the action itself, thereby bridging the gap between activity and accomplishment. It increases effortlessness and joy in the journey whilst minimizing potential burnout.

Delivering and Expressing Value

I had already utilized the system for a number of individuals, and believed that keeping value and relationships at the fore in combination with the above principles was essential to ongoing success.

I wanted to test this further now in view of previous challenges I had personally experienced in business. Here is a prime example.

When it came to business I struggled to truly value my gifts and talents for many years. I would often feel intimidated by aggressive practices I observed in the commercial world. What I wanted to do with my skills and talents did not seem to fit in with traditional categories of doing business, and for years I just tried to fit in with existing models.

Fundamentally that was an issue of self-esteem and ignorance. I did not realize it at the time. However, added to that was the fact that my leadership style was one of a servant leader. In other words I liked to lead by example through serving others. This was one positive aspect of my cultural background, and something I observed during my brief visit to the Fiji Islands.

During my stay in Fiji I was shown hospitality such as meal invitations, being given directions and a free lift by relative strangers when lost. The Fijian people were very sociable, ready and willing to assist without asking for remuneration. They were full of courtesy and respect, and treated me as an important person.

Even though the country suffered poverty, smiles were plenty, and the simple gestures of conversation and dialogue were returned with genuine smiles. These people had richness in their attitude and demeanor that I don't see so much in the West where materialism is more present.

Also I used to work in the service industry for many years in nursing, which was highly altruistic. It is understandable from the combination of the factors above that I would struggle to value myself in a business world that could be quite cut throat at times.

It was the lesson from football about playing big that was to help me change this. Then, I recall watching Arsenal playing in a cup game one day, and I got frustrated that they had so much possession without penetrating in the final eighteen yard area. There was no end product to their build up play.

It occurred to me that I was doing this in business. The moment I received that awakening, things progressed further. I rewrote some of my dreams in my dream journal, including the fact that I wanted to become 'sought after', based on high value delivery and credible reputation, just as I had experienced in nursing.

Ever since my nurse training I noticed that every post I held came about from being head hunted because of my high value delivery and accomplishments. I never campaigned for myself, yet my reputation spread. I wanted to see if I could repeat this in business.

I noticed an increase in confidence and courage to express the value and benefits of my new system, whether I was sharing with an individual, an executive, or a company. Serendipitous things then started to happen personally and professionally.

SERENDIPITY

Serendipity 1

I had barely finished putting the coaching system together when something happened…..

It had been a long standing dream of mine to work with football stars, and other sports stars in terms of coaching them on the inner aspects of their game. My passion for football and sport in general was undying.

I also wanted to work in an arena where my skills would be stretched, and where I could work in depth. I wanted to 'punch above my weight' so that I could get the best of myself and give the best to others – that's why I named my coaching company My Personal Best Coaching.

When I worked briefly with Tony Adams, I thought the dream might take off back in 2004, but for some reason it did not. I am not sure why, but I think there were many factors at work. It was quite rare back then for this type of coaching to be accepted so widely in the men's league even though there was much talk concerning the importance of mental preparation. Not many were as open to coaching as Tony was. Maybe I was too timid about pushing the coaching agenda forward in men's football given the resistance.

Now that I had developed a high value proprietary system, I wanted to test the universal laws at large, carry out my responsibility, and see what happened. I would simply share it and trust for doors to open.

A few months later, I was contacted to assist a friend of a friend with his business growth. I did some pro bono work on a consultancy basis, but must confess I did not pay too much attention to this person's business beyond his immediate need.

A few months later I was contacted by the same person I assisted, and was informed of the enormous value of my input. Shortly after, I discussed the emergence of my new coaching system, and was formally invited to work collaboratively with him, using my system, and other related skills – his industry covered commercial management in sports, music and film.

This put me in a position of indirect access to some of the top premiership football clubs as well as other sports industries, where I could share the benefits of my system to aid sports performance. Two things had happened here at once –an opportunity to share my system based on perceived value and credibility.

Secondly I had been sought after on this occasion, and now there was an opportunity to combine skill sets for greater value delivery to the industry. My colleague also shared a big humanitarian dream too – icing on the cake!!

Whilst this venture did not last more than a year, due to parting values, I had gained some crucial insights as to what was possible as well as what I was capable of achieving.

For example although my expertise was not in commercial contracts, my coaching delivery was met with high praise and endorsement. Many prospective clients reflected back on my timely communication skills as well as my grasp of underpinning values in that process.

A strong understanding of psychology and the mind enabled me to empathize and draw people out at a deeper level, such that they were able to feel valued. It gave me a strong context to articulate the benefits of coaching for mental preparation and performance in sports. This strength in developing rapport resulted in engaging prospects and bringing key relationships to the pool of potential resources needed to service clients. I came to appreciate these transferable skills as important leadership qualities too.

Serendipity 2

This one is very specific. I wanted to have the opportunity to collaborate with someone I considered to be one of the world's foremost brain wave entrainment specialists. I had personally been using his technology for years with great benefit.

A situation occurred several months later, where I had opportunity to opt to be a case study on his latest series. I did this and sent documented video feedback. He then asked for volunteer case studies in a particular category, so he could test out some customized tracks. I was able to provide this from my client list.

I got to use his technology in combination with my coaching. I had a ten year old female client who represented Great Britain in a gym event called tumbling. Her mother approached me for assistance, as fear was affecting her daughter's performance to the extent that she was losing control over her body. She had lost her medal status. At one point, she sprained her wrist badly during a warm up session, and was now ready to quit.

Within two weeks of using a part of my coaching system, which included a custom made brain wave entrainment track from my colleague, this young girl regained composure, eliminated physical issues and came top of her age category in the national tournament! She regained her medal status!

The thrill for me was working collaboratively with my colleague to deliver a personalized, high value process which enabled a young girl to overcome her fear and excel beyond her personal best with great results!

Serendipity 3

In line with my humanitarian dream I was head hunted to join a team involved in humanitarian contribution as part of a global initiative. The man that headed hunted me was a colleague of five years standing. At the time he was involved in a sports gym project, where he was trying to develop a health and wellbeing service to support fitness. We explored collaborative ideas based on my mental health expertise, as well as my sports knowledge.

He knew nothing of my humanitarian dream, and I knew nothing of his involvement until a chance conversation one day, while discussing other work. He alluded to a financial initiative he was part of which involved sophisticated investments and humanitarian contribution combined.

He had not mentioned anything before because he was quietly screening me as to my stature and character, with a view to inviting me onto the team. Sadly he died recently, yet once again seeds of possibility had been sown.

Serendipity 4

With regards this book, I felt strongly about wanting to write an inspirational song to accompany it. I used to write songs and sing, but my confidence on the singing front had dwindled as a result of strain on my vocal chords. My confidence issues were also due to past associations with church.

I decided to ask an empowering question during my meditative practice. I wanted to meet someone who had spiritual depth, understood inspiration, and who would help me with the writing and/or singing of the song. Several months later a strange event took place at 6am.

I had gone to bed at two in the morning, so it was unusual to find myself wide awake and alert at six o'clock after only four hours of sleep. I decided to get up. I usually start the day with meditation and some form of personal development practice before commencing any work.

However on this occasion I found myself doing something out of routine. I switched my computer on, went straight to my email inbox, and clicked on one of the 'peace' newsletters I had subscribed to. I hadn't opened any newsletters for quite some time, so this was strange enough.

I was immediately drawn to a music video of a mother and daughter singing the famous song 'when you believe'. This was a song I knew, and it was beautifully sung, but there was something that was drawing me to listen to it repeatedly. I must have listened to it twelve times consecutively that morning.

I had goose bumps every time I listened, and I knew instinctively that it was not just because a favorite inspirational song was being sung well. Before I consciously understood what I was doing, I reached out to connect to the mother via Facebook. Her name was Ana.

I expressed my gratitude for the singing and sharing of the song, and then shortly afterwards I asked if I could discuss a potentially mutual project – I was thinking of my song, and I acted instinctively.

Thankfully she replied, and the rest is history. When we spoke on skype, everything I had picked up by intuition got confirmed when Ana shared something of her journey, along with her vision. The spiritual connection was strong. We spoke a similar language, with mutual understanding and expression of spiritual values.

Beyond any immediate expectation, a beautiful friendship sprung out of that too. The other thing I experienced through repeated viewing of the music video, and then a symbol Ana shared, was the message of a theme that had played out in my life which I had almost forgotten about.

The message and the theme was around the concept of 'moving mountains', and part of that song kept resounding within me - 'we were moving mountains long before we knew we could'.

It felt like waves of memories were flooding back and washing over me about where I had moved mountains through overcoming and achieving the seemingly impossible at various points of my life. I also felt a hint of future things to come on a larger scale, though was not sure what.

Some of the memories that came flooding back with force, included:-

11yrs to 18yrs - putting winning hockey teams together at middle school, being the first female footballer to be asked to play in the boys team at middle school, passing my A levels first time, even though I had reportedly missed too much of the course to pass, due to a bout of shingles in my eye.

30yrs onwards - winning a landmark student appeal at nursing college, uncovering the murder from a dream, the first player to win three consecutive 'player of the season' trophies at the club, winning difficult industrial relations cases for nurses.

I also recall my brain wave entrainment colleague sensing and sharing that I would 'move mountains'! That was in late 2009. He had no idea of the significance of his words when he said it!! As if to confirm the flood of these memories, the next day I received a card from a friend with a picture of a mountain.

I now had someone to help me revive my singing in line with the song for my book. It turned out that Ana also had overlapping dreams and complementary skill sets, which we were both excited to explore further after our books were finished, with a view to working together.

Intuition and serendipity had opened the door of support and friendship. However, beyond that I sensed that a divine appointment had taken place, the significance of which would continue to unfold in time.

I had not been able to write a song for many years, yet strangely, after writing this book the lyrics and melody for the song came at a most unlikely moment. The last time I sneezed so violently I put my back out. This time when I went down with the common cold accompanied by heavy sneezing, I came out with a song in line with the theme of the book.

It underlined for me in a powerful way, how things can happen even when I am not at my physical best. I simply kept an open mind and trusted my intuition and my heart to assist in this matter.

These are just a few examples of how opportunities and people found me serendipitously, as I aligned with my core values and sought to create and deliver that value expansively. Even as I write this, some more amazing things are unfolding. I shall save these for another day, or even another book. They are too extraordinary to keep to myself.

Epilogue

A Call To Living

I want your life to be on the UP. More importantly I want you to live an inspired life. The current economic crisis is not the only crisis going on. Many are experiencing crisis in their emotional state and nearing a state of mental and spiritual bankruptcy.

There is a cry for people of value to impart real value in a way that inspires others to be the best they can be, and to live. Perhaps there is no moral obligation to give. However unless value is created and expressed there can be no greater value in the world.

I wanted my life to be of value to others through inspiration, rather than mere words. That meant I had to give myself the gift of value and inspiration first - it is easy to inspire from that place. In fact it is the only valid place from which inspiration can take place.

I used to work in perinatal psychiatry nursing mothers who suffered from post-natal illness, as a result of which the bonding process towards their newborn was difficult. I had come round full circle to the understanding that I needed to bond and reconcile with myself at heart level.

This would form the basis for true growth and living. Only from that place of connection could I discover purpose in my life that would find meaningful expression.

Through the process of knowing, choosing, developing and expressing, we can journey from becoming a best friend to becoming a true leader in our own lives. From that place of fulfillment and success, others can be inspired likewise.

'When you rob yourself of all you can be, you are like a
thief in the night'

A Narayan

One of the most inspirational movies I have ever watched is 'The Shawshank Redemption'. This is the story of one of the greatest prison escapes by the film character Andy Dufreyne who was wrongly imprisoned for the murder of his wife.

Morgan Freeman stars as one of the inmates. His famous speech on institutionalization summed up the true nature of imprisonment...

'At first you hate them, [prison walls] then you get used to them... enough time passes....you get so you depend on them'

Many live within an inner prison, devoid of dreams or life purpose, and secure if not free, as a result of the conditioning informed by their life experiences. They love the idea of life beyond survival, but don't think they can make it on the outside of their own prison.

They believe their prison can only be unlocked by circumstance or someone else, when really all along they hold the key. They don't know any different.

At the end of the day there is a difference between passing through survival and dwelling there. None of us are immune from having to survive at times. However, the longer you dwell in survival mode the more conditioned you become by it.

I have discovered that when you rob yourself of all you can be, you are like a thief in the night; a thief because you deny yourself your value and the joy of your human potential, and in so doing, you steal from yourself; a thief in the night, because you are asleep to the fact that you are robbing yourself.

Do not deny yourself the gift of life. Decide to form that nexus of true self-reconciliation. Decide to break free from your prison and find that place called living. Bring those unexpressed or aborted dreams off the shelf.

If you find yourself stuck in survival, ask an empowering question about the awakening and inspiration needed to set yourself free. You don't have to be religious; you just have to be open. This process is no discriminator of persons. It is not discretionary. It is your inheritance.

Ask as if you mean it. Your inner readiness will set of a chain of events that will deliver your solution. When it does, you too will discover that the key to your life was in your hands all along.

One thing I do know. If you fail to awaken and rise to your potential, if you fail to express your unique gifts while on this earth, then I and others are all the poorer for it. We are denied the abundance it brings to every area of our lives.

When you do the opposite, I am all the wealthier for it and the sharing of your gifts allows me to soar to new heights. This book is a personal response to that call. I didn't want to write this book back in 2004, because my need to hold on to what little privacy I had restored was so strong.

However in time the desire to bring value out of darkness and inspire others became stronger, and so this is my gift to you. I came alive in the dark constraint of my prison and I broke free. So can you!

May this book provide a roadmap to help you do that as well. May it inspire you to believe that if it can be done, then you can do it too. May the song I have written transport you a thousand miles on that journey. I hope to meet you some day in the land of the living. The world needs a community of people who are truly 'alive'. There is plenty of room in this land for you.

In the words of Andy Dufreyne …

'I guess it comes down to a simple choice really…get busy living or get busy dying'

On a note regarding the sheer beauty of living, my nephew recently wrote to share that he had journeyed to a point of discovering and accessing the joy of self-acceptance and happiness from within. This is another dream come true for me.

Moments like this underline the purpose and message of self-reconciliation in this book. It is one of the greatest wonders of the world to behold the beauty of growth that comes when the human spirit frees itself up to discover and embrace life. It is the core theme of my life's work now.

The great thing about this place called living is that there is no point of arrival. There are horizons, and when you come to the end of all you think you know and have discovered, you find a starting point for new horizons.

I recall from my attendance at the Life Mastery University, how Tony Robbins talked about a business adversary who had wronged him. He oddly referred to this person as being a 'worthy opponent' because Tony had to grow and become bigger than the situation to triumph.

When I started out on this journey, my view of my father was as an opponent whom I needed to defeat. My breaking free from my inner prison was so that he would not win. However, as my journey progressed, I shed that competitive perspective.

Ultimately for me, my father's actions and subsequent imprisonment had provided a mirror in which I was able to observe the full spectrum of own my imprisonment, and the potentially fatal consequences of not breaking free. It gave me a reference point to the potential for living free.

The unpleasant actions of my father and the trauma of my upbringing ultimately caused me to grow and find myself, as a person in my own right. In so doing, it caused me to find higher ground.

My father's imprisonment had forced me to look at my own prison and set myself free. His life sentence has now caused me to begin my own life sentence – the sentence and mandate to live!

I had been introduced to a whole new ball game as a result of the storm that broke out in my life. It is called living.....and to that I say 'game on!'

...to be continued!!

Further Information

Thank you for reading this book and its message. I hope that it has inspired you and provided you with stepping stones to translate into your journey. I would love to hear back from you as to what inspired you if you feel able and willing. This will help me by way of feedback as well as to share and spread inspiration further.

You can leave a comment or review at my website. You can also leave a review at Amazon which will help others who may be considering purchase.

Should you require or need further assistance with translating the essential lessons in the book, please feel free to reach out to me via my website. I look forward to serving you

www.Breaking-Free.co

www.AnitaNarayan.com